In the Garden of Myrtles

SUNY Series in Muslim Spirituality in South Asia
Annemarie Schimmel, Editor

In the Garden of Myrtles

Studies in Early Islamic Mysticism

Tor Andrae

Translated from the Swedish
by Birgitta Sharpe

Foreword
by Annemarie Schimmel

Biographical Introduction
by Eric Sharpe

STATE UNIVERSITY OF NEW YORK PRESS

Translated from the Swedish *I myrtenträdgården: Studier i tidig islamisk mystik* First published by Albert Bonniers Forlag in 1947. Re-issued by Bokforlaget Doxa AB. Lund 1981 as Doxa Reprint Number 7, ISBN 91-578-0112-6. This reissue follows the second edition of 1947 and forms the basis of this translation.

Published by
State University of New York Press, Albany

Printed in the United States of America

For information, address State University of New York
Press, State University Plaza, Albany, N.Y., 12246

Library of Congress Cataloging in Publication Data
Andrae, Tor, 1885–1947.
In the garden of myrtles.

(Suny series in Muslim spirituality in South Asia)
Translation of: I myrtenträdgården.
Bibliography: p.
1. Sufism—History. I. Title. II. Series.
BP188.6.A5313 1987 297'4 86-30074
ISBN 0-88706-523-6
ISBN 0-88706-524-4 (pbk.)

10 9 8 7 6 5 4 3 2 1

CONTENTS

FOREWORD

Annemarie Schimmel

Sometimes wishes are fulfilled when one no longer expects it—times have changed, and the wish, ardent as it was, has become dormant. And then, the *ashraf as-sā^{c}āt*, the auspicious hour, suddenly appears, and one understands that the fulfillment of wishes has its own timing, as the Sufis of yore knew very well.

When Tor Andrae's book *I Myrtenträdgården* appeared in 1947, shortly after the learned author's death, I had just started teaching Islamic languages and culture; at the same time I was studying History of Religion with Friedrich Heiler, who was deeply influenced in his thought by the Swedish tradition. Being a great admirer of Andrae's earlier books, particularly his masterful study *Die person Muhammads in lehre und glaube seiner gemeinde* (1918), in which he shows the development of the veneration of the Prophet of Islam, I knew that I had to read this new publication, and therefore learned Swedish. When the book finally reached me in post-war Germany thanks to some generous Swedish friends, I found it even more fascinating than I had expected. I was hoping to translate it into German, but a German translation by Hans-Helmhart Kanus was published in 1960. After joining Harvard I felt that an English translation was greatly needed by my students in the classes on Sufism but I found no time to do it. That Birgitta Sharpe, during our meeting in Sydney, volunteered to translate the book and completed the translation just at the moment when my path led me back to Uppsala, was more than fortuitous.

Why was I so impressed by this rather slim book with its appealing title? I think it was because of the way the earliest strata of Sufism are represented here. As is well known, the study of Sufism began in Europe in the early nineteenth century, and the first work in the long line of publications, F.A.D. Tholuck's *Ssufismus sive philosophia persarum pantheistica* (1821) already shows in its title that the author takes Sufism to be a purely pantheistic worldview; it was always considered to be "a foreign plant in the sandy soil of Islam," as another nineteenth-century scholar wrote. We can forgive them, for the material that was at their disposal consisted mainly of Persian poetry and some theoretical writings of later Sufis; and it was, and still is, easy to see all the colorful images in Persianate Sufi poetry as expressions of the all-pervading Unity of Being, the unity that underlies everything in the world and leaves no room for the distinctions of good and evil, of slave and Lord, of faith and infidelity.

At a somewhat later stage in the nineteenth century, European scholars began to see the Sufi path as an Islamized version of Neo-Platonic ideas, that is, as something grown out of the conscious or unconscious adaptation of Gnostic and Hellenistic ideas, as much or as little as they might fit into the Islamic worldview. Given the fact that Neo-Platonic ideas were in the air, so to speak, in the Mediterranean areas where Christian and Jewish thinkers had elaborated them, it would be quite surprising if Islamic spirituality had not received a fair share of them. Greek philosophical works, in particular the so-called "Theology of Aristotle," a Neo-Platonic work, had been translated into Arabic in the ninth century, at a time when Sufi asceticism was developing in Iraq, Iran, and Egypt. However, the apophthegmata of the Sufi fathers show little, if any, interest in speculative theology yet are rather in tune with the ascetic currents in the neighboring areas of Central Asian Buddhism and Near Eastern Christianity. The figure of Dionysius Areopagita, so central to the development of medieval Christian mysticism, is unknown in the history of Sufism. Again, a more philosophically oriented attitude toward problems of mystical theology can be witnessed among the Sufis from approximately the tenth century onward; this culminates in the refined theosophical system of the Spanish-born Ibn ᶜArabī (d.1240) which was to become dominant in later Islamic mysticism and was spread into the Eastern Islamic countries mainly through the influential Sufi orders, which began to crystallize in the twelfth century to form a large network of spiritual centers between Bengal and Morocco. As earlier Western scholars had access only to comparatively late Sufi texts—whether poetry or theoretical prose—they interpreted Sufism as consisting of nothing but Neo-Platonic ideas in Islamic disguise. Furthermore, as the majority of the sources earlier known to European scholars were written in Persian or belonged to the Persianate world which comprises the areas between Istanbul and Muslim India, some scholars found in Sufism an "Aryan" protest against the dry Semitic core of Islam or saw in it a typical expression of 'Iranian' religiosity; there were also those for whom Sufism was only a slight variation of Indian mystical teachings.

It was in the great work of Louis Massignon about al-Ḥallāj, the famed martyr-mystic of Islam (executed in Baghdad in 922) that the Islamic roots of early Sufism were expounded for the first time. Although Massignon's enormous opus is somewhat colored by his very personal attitude to and experience of mysticism, yet it was and still is one of the most inspiring, though at times difficult, studies of classical Sufism. The figure of his hero, the martyr-mystic al-Ḥallāj, has indeed constituted a major theme for Sufis and non-Sufis alike to our day. Ḥallāj's word *Anā 'l-ḥaqq* "I am the Truth" was interpreted as 'I am God' and seen as a stringent proof for his pantheistic outlook; his death at the hand of the government was taken as the model of the martyrdom of those who fight and want to die for an ideal, be it religious or sociopolitical. In fact, the suffering Ḥallāj has become a symbol not so much for those who seek God and long for union with Him through death, but for those who have been imprisoned, killed, or tortured by unjust governments; for the free spirits who suffer from narrow-minded ultraorthodox leaders. Ḥallāj, who "wanted to bring resurrection to the spiritually dead" (as Muḥammad Iqbāl said) has therefore attracted much interest during the last fifty or sixty years, and his life and death, his tender poems and daring outcries have been interpreted time and again by representatives of the most different spiritual trends.

It is with the remembrance of this "landmark" that Andrae's book begins; Ḥallāj's death forms the starting point of his studies. However, he does not follow the development of this fascinating personality but rather leads the reader back to the beginnings of the Sufi movement. The overwhelming figure of the martyr-mystic had usually overshadowed the figures before him; it was only in later years—after Andrae's book, barely known outside Scandinavia—that some studies concerning the masters of the eighth and ninth centuries were undertaken: Josef van Ess's book on al-Muḥāsibī (1957), and the studies on Bāyezīd Bisṭāmī by Hellmut Ritter and R.C.Zaehner. Interest in the early leaders of the Sufi movement such as Dhū'n-Nūn, al-Ḥakīm at-Tirmidhī, Sahl at-Tustarī, al-Kharrāz, and last but not least al-Junayd, is slowly growing. An exception to the general neglect of the formative period of Sufism was Margaret Smith's book, *Rābiᶜa, The Mystic* (1928), which supplied much material about the role of women in early Islam. Andrae, too, deals with the ascetic attitude to women, for he leads the reader through the various attitudes of the Sufis in every aspect of life. He shows them as human beings who devoted themselves completely to the study of God's word, to the imitation of the Prophet, and whose main goal was ethical, not metaphysical—the struggle against the lower qualities of the self and their replacement by the noble qualities as manifested in God.

Thus the early Sufis emerge from Andrae's book as true representatives of what the history of religion calls 'voluntaristic mysticism' or 'mysticism of personality' and not, as the later sources would have us believe, as examples of 'mysticism of infinity'. The very personal relation of these pious men and women with God, the Lord and the Beloved, is strongly emphasized; thus, instead of a hagiography with numerous miracles and almost exchangeable traits of personality, we encounter here people who, in their searching and striving, in their absolute passion for God the One and His unity, appear so alive that we can feel their presence in our lives.

Andrae of course also deals with the relations of these early Sufis with their Christian neighbors. His earlier study *Zuhd und Mönchtum* (*Asceticism and Monasticism*) had discussed the links between anchoretic monasticism and certain types of Islamic asceticism. It goes without saying that the people who were seeking God knew of each other and worked together at some time; but for the Muslim ascetic, his own status is always superior to that of his Christian colleague, even though Jesus is shown in this tradition as the ideal lover of God and perfect ascetic. Andrae is able to evoke the fraternal love which was typical of many of the stern ascetics and contrasts so strongly with a self-centered interest in one's own salvation. We can sense how the roots of *adab* 'proper behavior' toward God and man and even animals begin to develop in the circles of these simple men and women for whom one of the greatest virtues in this world was "to prefer others to themselves." Their strong trust in God, *tawakkul* (a topic analyzed in detail by Benedikt Reinert in his well-known study of 1968), endears them to us, even though a modern reader may be slightly shocked by the intensity of their search and their abandonment of everything worldly for the greater glory of God. Andrae makes it clear that true religious experience is highly resistent to systematization; through his loving approach to these pious seekers of ancient times he proves what his teacher, Archbishop Nathan Söderblom, had emphasized throughout his life and repeated even at the moment of his death, that is that the Living God and His work can be understood through the study of the history of religions. It is the strength of the early Sufis' faith, their divine love, which made them witnesses to the Living God of Islam. And this is the secret that has been at the center of true Sufism from their time to our day.

About the Notes

As the manuscript of Tor Andrae's book was published posthumously, the footnotes were not checked properly, nor were they checked in the German translation of 1960. It is very easy to misread quotations in footnotes, and the author would have certainly caught some more inconsistencies. We have tried to check whatever seemed doubtful, as far as the books were at our disposal. Since Andrae used editions which are in part no longer in use, it was not always possible to ascertain the right reading. In very doubtful cases I have put a question mark in brackets [?] to alert to reader; in other cases I have substituted the correct reading, the mistake often caused simply by an inversion of numbers. The editor of the Swedish text, Professor Geo Widengren, had added a few remarks of his own, which are marked *GW*; the translator has given some explanations of names little known outside Scandinavia, and I have added in brackets a few recent titles for particular topics or figures.

BONN, JULY 8, 1986
THE 101st BIRTHDAY OF TOR ANDRAE

Tor Andrae

Eric Sharpe

In the academic study of religion during the past century, few European countries have made a more impressive contribution to scholarship than has Sweden. This has been especially marked in the field of comparative religion (or the history of religions), that is, the critical study of the religions of the world through their own forms of expression and free from Christian, or other, apologetical considerations. Beginning shortly after the turn of the century with the appointment of Nathan Söderblom to the chair of 'theological propaedeutics and theological encyclopedia' (for which we may perhaps be allowed to substitute 'comparative religion') in the University of Uppsala, the tradition has continued unbroken to our own day. However, not all its representatives have been equally well known outside Scandinavia. Today, in a world made small by jet travel, academic colleagues are able to meet one another fairly regularly, almost irrespective of their countries of origin. This was of course not always so, and in the past scholars became known almost entirely through what they were able to publish in one or other language of world communication—before 1939 generally German, French and English in that order. A scholar publishing mainly in a 'minority' language and travelling only to close-at-hand countries as a rule remained enclosed within a very small local professional guild.

There are two things to be said in connection with Tor Andrae. First, he provided the necessary link between the 'classical' and 'modern' periods of the study of religion in Sweden. His mentor was Nathan Söderblom, and among his disciples were several outstanding scholars of what is now the Swedish older generation. Second, the fact that he published chiefly in Swedish—only to a limited extent in German, and with the exception of one celebrated translation, not at all in English—has more or less guaranteed his subsequent obscurity outside northern

Europe. Hitherto the only of his books to find its way into the English language has been his study of Muhammad, first published in Swedish in 1930; and even then only by way of an earlier German translation. Most of his writings on Islamic subjects, this present book among them, have long been available in German, but that is of very little help to students in the English-speaking world these days. But Islamists acknowledge Andrae as one of the founding fathers of modern Islamic studies in the West, and that is one of the reasons for the appearance of this present volume. What is far less accessible outside Scandinavia is the very considerable body of his writings on other religious and cultural subjects, not least among them the psychology of religion, to which he in fact devoted a large part of his academic career, especially in the 1920s. Also there remains the fact that the Islamist Andrae was a deeply devoted Christian, for almost forty years a minister and for the last ten years of his life a bishop in the Lutheran Church of Sweden. In this connection he also wrote a great deal that inevitably has remained little known outside Sweden. All in all, his was a many-sided achievement, and his career one that is well worth recalling.[1]

Tor Julius Efraim Andrae was born on July 8, 1885 in the southern Swedish country parish of Vena, the eighth of nine children and the youngest of four sons of Rev. Anders Johan Andrae and his wife Ida Carolina (née Nilsson). At the time of his death at the relatively early age of 61, on February 24, 1947 he was Lutheran Bishop of Linköping, an office he had held since 1937. The years between he had shared between University and Church. Entering the University of Uppsala in 1903, he had graduated in Arts in 1906 and in Theology in 1909, in which year he was also ordained into the Lutheran ministry. He completed his Licentiate degree in 1912, and five years later, in 1917, published the work by which his name became internationally known among Islamists, *Die person Muhammeds in lehre und glauben seiner gemeinde.*[2] This gained him his position as *docent* (more or less the equivalent of associate professor) in Uppsala, though his doctorate was not in fact awarded until 1921. From 1923 to 1933 he taught the history of religions at what was then Stockholms Högskola (not yet officially a university). Elected in 1929 to the chair of the history of religions in Uppsala—that vacated by Nathan Söderblom in 1914 on his elevation to the Archbishopric of Uppsala—for several years Andrae taught in two universities concurrently. From 1933 to 1937 however he remained with only his Uppsala duties, with the exception of a few weeks in the summer of 1936 during which he served as Minister of Ecclesiastical Affairs in a short-lived Country Party (*Bondepartiet*) Government. And in 1937, as already noted, he became Bishop of Linköping.

Subsequent to his ordination in 1909 Andrae had served as his father's curate for a couple of years, after which he became assistant minister (*komminister*) in various country parishes. He remained an active minister until May 1928, by then having spent thirteen years (1915–1928) concurrently with his university responsibilities serving in the parish of Gamla Uppsala (Old Uppsala), a few miles to the north of the university and cathedral city. For nine years, from 1928 to 1937, he had no pastoral charge of his own, though in 1931 he had been close to being elected Archbishop of Uppsala on Söderblom's death; in the event the choice went elsewhere. During his ten years as Bishop of Linköping (1937–1947)—six of them under wartime conditions in some ways almost as difficult in Sweden as in Nazi-occupied Norway and Denmark—Andrae was far less of a scholar than he might have chosen to be. But in the last years of his life he was able to do as Söderblom had done in similar circumstances and deliver a final series of lectures in which he returned to the academic delights of earlier years. And as in Söderblom's case, Andrae was not to live to see his last lectures appear in print. Söderblom's *The Living God* (delivered as Gifford Lectures in Scotland) appeared only after his death. So too in this present case. *In the Garden of Myrtles*, comprising a series of Olaus Petri Lectures held in Uppsala in the spring of 1945, was published in Swedish later in the year of Andrae's death (1947); only now, exactly forty years later, do we have an English translation.

The name of Tor Andrae is, as I have said, well known among Islamists, thanks to a long sequence of publications, mostly in German, which appeared between 1912 and 1930, with this present work as a postscript. This side of his contribution Professor Annemarie Schimmel discusses separately elsewhere in this volume. There remains, however, the intriguing question of Tor Andrae himself, and of the relationship between Andrae the Arabist and Islamist and Andrae the Christian minister and bishop. To many, it is no doubt practically inconceivable that the same person could sustain both identities without the one exercising a destructive influence on the other. Or else it will be assumed that there operated some form of deliberate compartmentalization, Islam here and Christianity there, with the two kept apart by the tightest of bulkheads. However, to make either assumption would be to do Andrae—and for that matter the generation to which he belonged—a grave injustice. Nor will it do simply to dismiss one or the other of Andrae's identities, academic or religious, on the tactic argument that because it is unimportant or incomprehensible to the latterday critic, it cannot have been other than peripheral to Andrae himself.

Comparative religion as taught in Uppsala in the years before the first world war was not without a certain element of Christian apologetics. Mostly, however, it was a historical and philological discipline, based on the closest possible acquaintance with the relevant texts in the original languages. A further important element was provided by the newly found techniques of the psychology of religion, chiefly in the wake of the American investigators Hall, James, Starbuck and Leuba. This approach to religion was of course far more individual than collective (in later years Andrae remained skeptical of collective interpretations of religion in general, and of the theories of Durkheim in particular), and had a special focus of interest in the phenomena associated with mysticism—a subject close to Andrae's heart, as we shall see.

Andrae's teacher Nathan Söderblom was not an expert in Islam. Andrae for his part had begun in his undergraduate years to cultivate a detailed study of Semitic languages as part of a necessary background to the study of the Old Testament, very much in the tradition of William Robertson Smith. Chief among those languages, aside from Hebrew, was Arabic. So it was that in 1909, having just graduated in theology, Andrae was summoned to Söderblom's room and asked, to his astonishment, whether he wanted to become a lecturer in comparative religion. He stammered something about not being qualified, only to be interrupted by Söderblom: "That was not what I asked. I am asking you whether you *want* to!" It was, then, Söderblom who directed Andrae to investigate the understanding of the person of Muhammad as held by the earliest Muslim communities—as Widengren has said, a happy accident, a result of Söderblom's brilliant intuition.[3]

At this time Andrae may not have been qualified to teach comparative religion. He was on the other hand well equipped, temperamentally as well as academically, to acquire the necessary qualifications. His close friend H.S. Nyberg wrote in 1947:

> Growing up in a country vicarage was of fundamental importance to Tor Andrae the historian of religion. It is perhaps the best preparatory school there is for the historian of religion in the making. In the vicarage the child is able to make the acquaintance, daily and personally, of the realities of religious life. Superstition, still very much alive in the Swedish countryside at the turn of the century, and still by no means extinct, is discussed in the vicarage in connection with actual cases, is analysed and evaluated, and the child also encounters it outside and sometimes inside the vicarage walls—often the maids were excellent transmitters of tradition. Popular customs and practices become familiar from childhood. The ways of thinking about and reacting to life and the environment, which characterize

> country people and which it is so important for the historian of religion to know at first hand, if he is to be able to evaluate analogous stages of culture—all this the child received as a free gift, it becomes a living part of his world of ideas. These are things that never can be learned from books; and those who pursue the history of religion only from the study desk make horrible elementary mistakes, explicable only as a result of their lack of contact with normal simple country people, their lives and ideas.[4]

Mention of Andrae's vicarage childhood however brings us back to the question of his Christian faith. I do not propose to deal with this in any detail, save to say that it was the faith neither of pietist revivalist nor of the confession-bound orthodox professional theologian (which Andrae was not). In private he was generally reticent on the subject, while in the pulpit he had an unconventional style, notably free from sentimentality and what used to be called 'unction'. To quote H.S. Nyberg again, Andrae's sermons ". . . captivated through their deep psychological understanding and perhaps chiefly through the fact that they came from a struggling man who was struggling with us and for us."[5] The depth of his scholarship notwithstanding, Andrae was a man of the people for whom all truly great things are basically simple, and therefore capable of being understood best by the simple people of this world—whether in Sweden or the Middle East mattered little. In himself he was neither a mystic nor an ascetic, except perhaps in the disciplined use of time: already as a student his capacity for rapid and totally concentrated study was well developed, and this ability never left him. In all he did he was always, directly or indirectly, a consummate educator as well as a determined inquirer into the innermost nature of religious experience.

This indeed was the scarlet thread running through almost the whole of Tor Andrae's later scholarly work. It is noteworthy that his well-established reputation as an Islamist notwithstanding, during the 1920s and 1930s he published far more in the area of the psychology of mysticism, and of religious experience generally, than in pure Islamics. In 1923 we find him lecturing on 'Speaking in tongues and faith healing,' and over the next few years there appeared in print further lectures on 'New mystical and apocalyptic religious movements,' 'Mysticism and society,' 'Psychoanalysis and religion' and a massive book in Swedish on *The Psychology of Mysticism: Possession and Inspiration* (Stockholm, 1927). Possibly it is true to say that had this appeared in English, French or German it would have become a standard work. Alas, it did not—added to which, it appeared completely devoid of footnotes and references to its many questions, rendering translation virtually impossible.

Those who write or attempt to write about the way of the mystics as virtuosi of the spiritual life may of course do so for more than one reason. There are those who have discovered the way for themselves, and desire nothing other than to guide others through its various stages. But there are others (and numerically one suspects that they will always be in the majority) who see in mysticism less a way to be followed than a puzzle to be resolved. There would seem to have been little enough of the mystic in Andrae's own personality. On the contrary, he was a man of the intellect and the will, a scholar through and through, who nevertheless devoted the greater part of his life to the theory and practice of religion, and within its wide frontiers especially to the investigation of mysticism—the way of religion elevated to the highest point of experience. In an essay on 'Mysticism and society' published in 1926 in a *Festschrift* for Nathan Söderblom, Andrae stated plainly his own personal preference for the 'Franciscan' type (that this essay was published in the year in which the Christian world was celebrating the seven hundredth anniversary of the death of St. Francis of Assisi in 1226 was doubtless fortuitous) over those 'experts and virtuosi of love' and 'heroes and masters of asceticism' who had previously occupied the center of the mystical stage.[6] The Franciscans were 'the geniuses of real love,' many of the others being mere *Geltungsbedürftige*, men and women with "a marked taste for the calculated, the remarkable, for that which lies beyond what is humanly possible."[7] In comparison with such virtuosi, the daily work of the normal householder may be all the more worthy of respect. It is clear from Andrae's writings on mysticism in general (of which his work on Islamic mysticism was only a part) that in the face of its varied phenomena he felt compelled to steer a difficult course between respect and skepticism; least of all did he give everything classifiable as 'mysticism' his unqualified approval. There was in fact a broad streak of skepticism in his own nature, and it was in a way only natural that he should also inquire—both as a historian and a psychologist—into the way of the skeptic alongside that of the mystic.

Andrae's 80-page monograph *Die Frage der religiösen Anlage religionsgeschichtlich beleuchtet* (1932) took up the question of the history, not of religion, but of irreligion, under the heading of the much-discussed 'religious instinct' so often claimed by the comparative religionists of the time to be a universal element of human experience. Andrae's argument, broadly speaking, was that the individualization and privatization of religion makes it inevitable that some individuals will opt out of religion altogether, and this he illustrated from primal, Nordic, Greek, Israelite and Indian sources. This work is still well worth reading.

The death of Nathan Söderblom in July 1931 gave Andrae the opportunity to demonstrate his gifts as a biographer. Before the year was out, his warm and exemplary Söderblom biography had been published (on the basis of lectures begun in the previous year), together with an excellent essay on 'Nathan Söderblom as a historian of religion' in the volume *Nathan Söderblom in memoriam* (also 1931). Two years previously, in 1929, Andrae had been appointed to the Uppsala chair once occupied by Söderblom, and in 1932 he was elected as one of the eighteen members of the Swedish Academy, again as Söderblom's successor.

It was under the auspices of the Academy that Andrae published in 1934 a second biographical essay, a study of Bishop Georg Wallin (1686–1760). Professionally Andrae was of course not an ecclesiastical historian, but it is amply evident from this elegant and carefully crafted study that he could well have been, had he so chosen. The ideas and ideals of the eighteenth century appealed to him greatly—witness a passage in which he apostrophizes the qualities of those scholars of the period who brought together sound religion and sound scholarship. Andrae speaks with warmth, and perhaps with a certain nostalgia, of those:

> . . . learned ministers of the old school, who knew their classics, delivered orations in Greek and Hebrew and with razor-sharp arguments refuted every known and unknown heresy. They have not always received full justice. When the great popular revival came with its gospel of religious introspection they were left standing there in their empty churches. There was no longer any understanding of the rough manly generosity of their church-centred Christianity. Schoolboys shrugged their shoulders at their dogmatics, which had been built up with such impressive intellectual effort and learning. And yet they had their great day. In its completeness and its power to dominate society their system was an achievement which since then has never been surpassed. In poverty and in hard times they kept the torches of knowledge burning—we who have the whole of our learning at hand in reference books and convenient library catalogues are put to shame when we reflect on the effort it must have cost them. They represented the proudest intellectual tradition Sweden possesses, the Protestant Enlightenment, the Magna Carta of which is Gustavus Adolphus' letter of donation to Uppsala University, which rests on the conviction that the University as a free republic, independent of the favours of rulers, should be the firmest foundation for 'the growth and maintenance of the Word of God and good politics in our country'. For Gustavus and the age that began with him, the highest values of life—the wellbeing of the land under

> orderly government, a true Christian Church and the highest learning and education—were inseparable. Hitherto we have too often concentrated on one side of the old Protestant educational ideal: the demands of the Church to be allowed to imprison and direct scholarship according to the narrow standards of the Lutheran confessions. It is far too easy to forget the other side, which is no less important: its irresistible conviction that a Church having no firm links with learning and study is unworthy and unable to fulfil its spiritual task as an educator.[8]

Both by instinct and accomplishment Tor Andrae was a historian, and to the historical instinct even his far-reaching psychological studies took second place. Whatever his field of interest, Islamic, Christian or 'comparative', it was as a psychologically trained historian that he approached his material. He would seem to have reflected only in private on the methodological problems involved in the study of religion, but in a letter to a friend (written in 1924) he revealed something of the perplexity the enterprise had caused him. He wrote:

> I might perhaps claim to call myself a historian, since I work with a certain kind of history, and I have often puzzled over what basically distinguishes historical method from what we have grown accustomed to call exact science, without succeeding in finding a comprehensible way of formulating the answer. I know that as historians we have to evaluate, and not merely describe. But by what criteria? And why do we then claim to have our results accepted as scientific? On the other hand I have a very strong feeling that I judge a historical context with a quite different degree of objectivity than I apply to a question of values, or an aesthetic question, in which I am personally involved. Although I really *am* subjective as a historian, I have a feeling that I do not *want* to be, or that I *ought* not to be . . . .[9]

It is perhaps worth recalling once more that it was as a historian and subsequently as a psychologist that Tor Andrae approached even the Islamic material—with the incidence of psychological reflection becoming more marked in later years, and especially so in this present work. The reader of this book will undoubtedly be struck by the degree of (for the most part unobtrusive) psychological reflection these pages contain. Similarly with Andrae's well-known study of Muhammad, which first appeared in Swedish over half a century ago, in 1930. There he begins by pouring some well-deserved scorn on that type of scholarship which ignored creative individual personalities in the history of religion, preferring instead to speculate on the collective process; there is, he pointed out, no great methodological virtue in imagining history as a drama without actors in the leading roles, a play consisting entirely of non-speaking 'extras'. The power of religion, he urged, proceeds not from the masses but from the charismatic personality of the leader, pioneer and prophet—a feature that Andrae had observed in the sects of his day and that we continue to observe in the new religious movements of ours.

> The master, the prophet and his disciples—that is the cell from which there emerges new life in the world of religion. There is no reason for scholarship to stop short on encountering the individual personality, as though it were a supernatural entity, in face of which research must lay down its arms. To investigate the ways in which a new spiritual synthesis is created in the inner life of the genius or the prophet out of elements that perhaps were all there in the world around him, but in isolation and without the chance of coming together, is potentially an attractive field for research before the scholar tackles that which is genuinely new, the secret of creative spiritual life.[10]

After a fashion one may investigate such a charismatic leader purely on a basis of claims made on his (or her) behalf by disciples; one may resort to psychological techniques; but without a sense of what was historically possible or probable, understanding is going to prove at best elusive. Andrae was, as we have said, most of all a historian, but a historian for whom psychological technique was a valuable tool in the elucidation of historical probability. So with the Prophet—so too with his disciples, their scruples, their compulsions and their battles with conscience, so elegantly documented in the following pages.

We should perhaps remember that Andrae's specialization was in the early, and not the modern history of Islam; in the first interplay of Judaism, Christianity and Islam *in situ*, and not in subsequent religio-political conflicts, least of all those of the twentieth century. Further, it was as a historian, and not as an apologist, that he was able to demonstrate—entirely on the basis of textual material, combed through over and over again—degrees of dependence and probable influence. As a psychologist he was in a position tentatively to locate this material in a wider human context of personalities, traits, motives and aspirations. Even though this present work (which, let it be remembered, Andrae himself had no opportunity fully to revise) contains a few incidental side references to Christian themes, ideas and personalities, it is in no way an exercise in Christian apologetics. Andrae was quite capable of writing apologetics when the occasion demanded. Here, however, as in all his Islamic work, he writes simply with affection and respect, altogether avoiding the contortions to which the practice of advanced inter-religious dialogue has been known to lead.

If I may be permitted a moment of personal reminiscence, I still recall the purely aesthetic pleasure I experienced in the years around 1960 when I first discovered the writings of Tor Andrae—not in Islamics, for I was not then, nor am I now an Islamist—but first his 1931 biography of Nathan Söderblom and subsequently his volumes of essays, especially *Den gamla prästgården* (*The Old Vicarage*, 1940). The modern Swedish language has had few more consummate stylists than Andrae. The point is worth making, that in common with not a few scholars of his generation (though perhaps relatively few of ours), Andrae was able to communicate with a wide public at the highest literary, as well as the highest scholarly level. This was a very substantial part of his calling—to address not only his academic colleagues and students, but equally those whom Schleiermacher once labelled religion's 'cultured despisers,' not necessarily on Islam but on the deepest problems of human life.

For one whose first visit to Sweden took place eleven years after Andrae's death, and who made the acquaintance of his writings later still, to speak at length about his character would be an impertinence. But from what others have said about him it is evident that he was not a man who carried his heart on his sleeve, so to speak. Rather he would appear to have been reticent, if not actually shy, in the company of those he knew only slightly, while opening up among close friends (and especially so in academic circles, among those he trusted and respected). Seldom, if ever, did he seek the limelight, partly perhaps out of a fear of being caught off guard or ill-prepared. While he was in many ways a man of the people who respected the ordinary folk more than some of his academic colleagues, he remained an intellectual—though an intellectual more than usually aware that the academic profession can never exempt those professing it from concern for the great questions of life and death. This did not however mean that he was forever allowing his own struggle for faith (and no one can read his extensive Christian writings and imagine for one moment that he found the road of religion easy, or that he was ever tempted to 'take his ease in Zion'; for those who did, he had little respect) to intrude upon his scholarship. Faith and scientific inquiry he believed to move on different levels of the human heart and mind, arguing (and who is to say that he was wrong?) that the perennial problem of how the two are to be reconciled may reflect no more than a hopeless attempt to resolve a paradox that in human terms admits of no solution.

An academic colleague once expressed to Tor Andrae his admiration over the depth of his scholarship, at a time when he had already begun to gain an international reputation as an Islamist. Andrae's reply was altogether typical of the man:

> It is not as remarkable as it looks. Imagine a garden surrounded by a high fence. Once you get over the fence, you can pick whatever flowers you like.[11]

In the case the fence was the Arabic language. Some of the flowers he found and picked in the Sufis' 'garden of myrtles' are gathered here, in the pages that follow. May they delight the reader as they once so delighted the one who picked them.

PREFACE TO THE ORIGINAL SWEDISH EDITION

This book is based on a series of lectures given in Uppsala under the auspices of the Olaus Petri Foundation in the spring of 1945. The manuscript, which was delivered to the publishers in November 1946, had been typeset and was at the galley-proof stage a few weeks after Tor Andrae's death. Professor Geo Widengren, the author's friend and former student, kindly made his time and expertise available for a careful reading of the proofs and in particular of the references. For the fact that the book is now available in the error-free edition—in so far as this is ever possible—we are indebted to him.

STAFFAN ANDRAE
STOCKHOLM, APRIL 1947

INTRODUCTION

On March 26, 922—at the time of the year when the death of Attis, the god of fertility, was being celebrated in Rome and Christianity was recalling the passion drama in Jerusalem—in Baghdad an eccentric mystic, al-Ḥusayn ibn Manṣūr al-Ḥallāj was crucified. He had been accused of claiming to be God, and of teaching that the deity could permeate and take possession of human nature; he was also charged with using magic to work the miracles that were supposed to prove his divinity. His judges, proceeding with all the formal conscientiousness of which true lawyers are so proud, did not, however, consider that he ought to be condemned on the basis of these somewhat vague accusations, which were in any case contested by Ḥallāj himself. But since the death sentence had been decided upon before the trial even began, he was condemned to death under every appearance of justice, on the grounds that he had taken certain liberties with the ritual laws of Islam. He had taught that it was permissible not to fast in the month of Ramadan, provided that one fasted strictly for three days and on the fourth day ate only a few endives; and that one could save oneself the difficult, and for many impossible, pilgrimage to Mecca by performing the appropriate ceremonies at home.

The actual execution was organized in accordance with oriental taste, which requires that one should enjoy such a stimulating performance in small portions. First he was flogged, after which his hands and feet were amputated. Then he was nailed to a cross, on which he was left to hang until the following morning, when he was finally decapitated. Ḥallāj himself was apparently unaffected. When they took him out to the place of execution, he laughed till tears ran—or so the story goes. When they crucified him, all he said was: "In the moment of ecstasy all the lover desires is the One. To be alone with Him!"

This tragic event had a remarkable sequel about a thousand years later. A French Orientalist, Louis Massignon, happened to become interested in the Sufi martyr in a manner almost calculated to make one believe in the possibility of reincarnation. He gathered together every word about and by Ḥallāj. He combed every library in Europe and the Near East, following the traces of his hero in something like two thousand carefully recorded works from both East and West, and set himself to write his story. It became a massive and impressive work, nine hundred pages long, in which for the first time the origins and earliest history of Muslim mysticism was described. For its author's part, the main conclusion was that Ḥallāj is the finest flower of Muslim mysticism, unsurpassed in the depth and boldness of his thought on the one hand, and in the warmth and sincerity of his personal devotion on the other.[1]

Where value judgments of this kind are concerned, everything depends on the point of view adopted by the author. Was Origen a more noteworthy religious personality than the author of the Gospel of John? Ought Tauler to be placed above John of the Cross or Catherine of Siena as a mystic? Naturally a theologically well-developed form of piety stands higher, in some respects, than that kind of spontaneous and unreflecting faith that simply relates what it has seen and experienced, without reservations or repressions. Religion must be preserved and taught, and therefore has to be thought out and, in a sense, understood. This is the task of theology, and it cannot be avoided. But when speculation has done all that it can, when it has transformed simple rules and statements about the experience of God into the subtleties of scholastic systems, it may well be that from the religious point of view, theological developments have not marked a step forward—or not *only* a step forward—but also a step backward. In the sacrificial hymns of the Veda there is both fresh nature-poetry and genuine worship. The Vedic speculations of the Brāhmanas, on the other hand, present to us a world as barren and petrified as a moonscape, fantastic without fantasy, as full of pretentious professional religion as they are empty of living piety. Sometimes the relationship between theology and religion is like that. It is when experience loses its living warmth, its healthy preoccupation with the present moment, that faith has the opportunity to retreat into speculation about its own nature and launches into detailed descriptions of the life of the soul. The self-conscious philosophy of love cultivated by the madrigalists of the late Renaissance appears to us largely as the record of a love that had lost its fresh complexion and its red blood. The mystics' love of God conveys much the same impression. It has had its living and creative poets, but also its systematizers, who have contrived in the fullness of time to organize and classify the dried flowers that once grew in the garden of the soul. The danger of theology ceasing to be a help in the understanding and experience of religion, or in Tegnér's words, of being a human skull covering up a lily, seems to me never to be more real than in the case of mysticism.[2] The inner world with which it is concerned is always highly resistant to theological systematization. Experiences which are meaningful in the context of only one life which will never be relived in the same terms; words and phrases which originally were fundamentally untranslateable expressions of individual impressions—these the systematizer attempts to transform into universally valid stages on an imaginary *scala mystica*, or into technical terms for experiences that everyone ought to be able to recognize and share. The result is a distortion of reality. Personally I have found the study of the theoreticians and the systems of mysticism to be for the most part a pilgrimage through the deserts.

The classical Sufi mystics also had an acute dislike of mystical speculation. "When God favours his servant, he opens to him the gate of good works and closes the gate of theological discussion," said Ma'rūf al-Karkhī.[3] And Ḥallāj's contemporary, the celebrated teacher of orthodox mysticism, Junayd, explained: "The least harm that theological speculation does is to take away the reverence of God from one's heart. And when the heart is empty of reverence, it is empty of God."[4] He did not conceal his feelings about Ḥallāj himself. When Ḥallāj in his mystical ecstasy broke with his former friends, he came to Junayd and asked to be reinstated as his disciple; to which Junayd answered roughly: "I don't associate with madmen. Association demands sanity, and if that is wanting the result is behaviour like yours."[5]

Of course there is nothing to prevent a theologian from being pious. He may be more than than; in some cases he may not be only an independent thinker but an original and creative religious personality. Ḥallāj was one of these great exceptions. But he represents a landmark in the history of Sufi mysticism. For him the path leads to that comprehensive theosophical mysticism in which the great name is that of Ibn al-'Arabī, whose works, though of great interest to the historian of religion on account of the way in which they have preserved so much of the lost world of Hellenistic mysticism, are in religious terms a barren desert, or perhaps rather a pathless fog. Also from him proceeds another path, in the direction of a mystical self-apotheosis, to the worship of the personality of the chosen spiritual leader, which was so notable a feature of the later sectarian religion of the Dervishes. The mystical sectarian leader, the sheikh, who is the living incarnation of the deity and who directs the faithful, often with the exercise of brutal power, more often with a refined form of spiritual tyranny, and sometimes even with simple tricks, is without doubt one of the most unattractive characters known to the history of religion.

I first made the acquaintance of Sufism in a more personal way along a path quite different from that of the theological systems. There came into my hand a book by a learned fourteenth-century collector, al-Yāfiʿī: *Rauḍ al-rayāḥīn fī manāqib al-ṣāliḥīn,* (*The Garden of Myrtles: Concerning the Virtues of the Pious*), or, in a rough attempt to reproduce the melodious rhymed prose of the original: "The garden filled with blossoms' fragrance—To every virtue of the faithful a remembrance." At the Kaʿba the Prophet Muhammad met a Beduin, whose simple piety impressed him greatly. In the midst of their conversation Gabriel came down to the Prophet with a revelation from God: "Say to the Beduin: 'Your trust in My grace and mercy will not help you, for tomorrow I shall call you to account over great things and small, even unto the raffia rope and the string of the wineskin.' Then said the Beduin, 'Shall my Lord indeed call me to account?' – 'Indeed He will call you to account, if it is His will to do so.' – 'By His might and majesty! If He calls me to account for my sin, I will call Him to account for His generosity . . .' Then the Prophet wept until his beard became wet. But Gabriel descended with a greeting from God. 'Weep not, Muhammad! The angels who carry My throne forgot for a moment their songs of praise out of pure joy. Say to your brother the Beduin that if he does not call Me to account, neither will I call him to account."[6] There was a tone in this naive story that impressed me greatly. I had myself heard simple men try to interpret, in similar terms, the challenging paradox of divine forgiveness, beyond all reason and all legalism. And soon I discovered that this was an imaginative reconstruction of some words of one of the great teachers of early Sufism, Abū Sulaymān ad-Dārānī.

Earlier Western writers on the subject of Sufism have generally concentrated on the ineffable merging of the believer and God, expressed so brilliantly by the great Persian poets—the description of the lover's way to that final union in which the soul, intoxicated by the drinks from the goblet of love and blinded by light eternal, senses how its own nature disappears and merges in the Loved One, the Only One. But I had become interested in Abū Sulaymān, his contemporaries and his successors. I collected their words and sayings, quoted by Sufi historians and theoreticians as *dicta probantia*, and I did so with the growing sense that what was religiously central, the creative impulse in the whole of this fascinating episode in the history of mysticism, was there in these forthright apostles and saints of the love of God.

In point of fact Islamic mysticism had already reached its pinnacle in religious terms by the time of Ḥallāj, as the great names of the orthodox mystics, Dhū'n-Nūn, Muḥāsibī and Junayd bear witness. A remarkable development took place during a period of 150 years, between

750 and 900 AD, or between 150 and 300 in Islamic chronology. An earlier ascetic piety, with its rough and gloomy eschatology, its contempt for this world and its rigid discipline, was interiorized through a living, burning love of God and deepened through the discovery of the soul's way to union with God and to the likeness of God through transformation according to His image. It is this development that is summarized and codified in Ghazālī's great work *The Revivification of the Science of Faith*. This brought Muslim piety to a high point beyond which it has never been able to pass and which it has unfortunately been unable to maintain.

This is a book about those 150 years, and about its leading figures, the classical writers of Sufi mysticism. In choosing this subject, I have been assailed not only with doubts but also with genuine anxiety, since it seems to me almost irresponsible to attempt to arouse interest in something so incredibly remote from the present day. Would that I had been able to produce shards of pottery or fragments of sculpture from some long-forgotten culture! But what we have is not only a matter of fragments of thought, or of what people believed and prayed for and hoped in a country and period far removed from ours. My hope is to bring to life a vanished world of religion, and this in a time when it is hard enough to interest people in religious questions belonging to the present day.

Nevertheless, I have made the attempt. I have done so because these persons captured my attention and fascinated me from the first moment I encountered them. Reading their words, I have had the strange experience of something at one and the same time new and strange, and yet familiar. I have looked into the face of a stranger, and found a friend. I have encountered sayings that have forced me to think afresh about my own faith. I have seen rays from a source of light that I know well, though here refracted through a new prism. Perhaps I dare to say that I have had an experience—albeit of more modest dimensions—like that which must have been in Nathan Söderblom's mind when, on his deathbed, he summed up his work as a historian of religion: "I know that God lives. I can prove it through the history of religion."

Chapter I

ISLAM AND CHRISTIANITY

Strange and yet familiar. This suggests a problem which, to myself, has been perhaps the most crucial during these studies. For a long time, research has simply passed it by. Scholars felt that such an exquisite flower as Sufi mysticism could not really have grown in the meager soil of Islam. They sometimes referred to the Persians, who were assumed to have had some kind of inborn penchant for mystical piety. They guessed at influences from India, from Buddhism and Vedānta. Or they thought of Neoplatonic mysticism, which at least could be studied in documents written in Arabic. Massignon's brilliant investigations have, at a single stroke, made these tentative speculations seem strangely anachronistic and out of date. He has shown that Sufism has grown in the ground of Islam, spirit of its spirit and word of its word. The mystical experience has emerged from and has found its way during incessant study of the Qur'an, and both its technical expressions and its issues are generally taken from the Qur'an. Step by step we are able to follow how this view has developed. One generation of pious men have stretched out their hands to another and even such wide-ranging and from Islam's point of view such controversial teachings as those of Ḥallāj can be traced back, according to Massignon, to their original source and their roots in purely Muslim ground.

This is, without doubt, correct. And more than that: this is what should be said, first of all, concerning the origins of Sufism. A couple of decades ago, research in the history of religions saw it primarily as its task to trace influences and effects from other religions in much the same way as literary scholars applied all their powers of detection to the contents of poets' libraries and which books they borrowed, in order to demonstrate what they must have read or at least might have read. It is an important aspect of the scholarly task, but it is not the only one, nor is it the most important one. The most important thing, that which decides whether the whole subject is worth the research scholar's trouble and effort, is not, after all, what a religion or its prophet has borrowed from others, but what he himself was, such influences notwithstanding. The most important concern is to penetrate to the source of poetry and creativity in his own being.

And yet Massignon has not solved the question of Sufism and Christianity. Their mutual relationship is more complicated than he appears willing to concede. If the Qur'an is the ground of mysticism, then Qur'anic piety itself builds, in important ways, on Christian foundations. Scholars nowadays doubtless largely agree that, from a certain point of view, Qur'anic piety can be regarded as a translation into Arabic language and Arabic imagination of that ascetic piety, that monastic religion, which flourished within the Syrian churches of the period. In this case, too, the decisive fact is however that the translation was carried out by a personality whose religious creativity one ought not to underestimate: Muhammad, the Apostle of Allah.

But the contact between Islam and Christianity had not come to an end when the faithful had received their Qur'an and no longer needed to feel envious of Christians on account of their holy scriptures. The Arabic conquest showed great gentleness toward the Christian population in the subjugated countries. The Christian churches could hardly complain. In 650 AD the head of the Nestorian church was able to write: "These Arabs do not only avoid fighting Christianity, they even endorse our religion, they honour our priests and holy men and donate gifts to monasteries and churches."[7] This surprising piece of information, that priests and monks had been particularly favored by the conquerors, is certainly not a mere invention. In Egypt, the monks were initially in fact entirely exempted from paying taxes, including the personal tax which every Christian and Jew had to pay in order to enjoy religious freedom. This policy of amity toward Christianity was in effect completely in accordance with the Prophet's own basic guideline in the Qur'an:

> Thou wilt surely find the most hostile of men to the believers are the Jews and the idolaters; and thou wilt surely find the nearest of them in love to the believers are those who say 'We are Christians'; that, because some of them are priests and monks, and they wax not proud . . . (*Sura* 5:85).

Thus Christians and Muslims lived together in peace for a long time. The semi-barbarian conquerors initially were forced to learn from the Christians, step by step, how to look after and administer their new dominions. Naturally they also heard a great deal about their religion. In the mountains, on the border between cultivation and the desert, the Christian hermit lives in his cell, built of greyish white bricks. As a rule the holy man is misanthropic and timid as a wild animal. But if one is fortunate, one may see him looking out through the narrow window of his cell. One calls out to him, with a mixture of respect and curiosity, and tries to draw him into conversation. What in the world do these people really want, those who adopt this style of life? There are innumerable instances of religious conversations between a monk or hermit, a *rāhib*, and one of the faithful. Here one encounters the difficulty that Muslim ascetics have, on occasion, also been called *rāhib*[2]. But the epithet is always used in an adapted sense. The monk, *rāhib*, is a foreign, non-Arabic phenomenon. He belongs in the context of Christianity. Muslim ascetics, as far as I have been able to ascertain, have never applied that term to themselves. The word is used by outside observers who have been struck by the similarity between the ascetic and ritual exercises of the faithful and the practices of the Christian monks. Abū Bakr ibn 'Abd ar-Raḥmān, because of the great extent of his praying, was called the *rāhib* of Quraysh[3]. Mālik ibn Dīnār was called the *rāhib* of the Arabs,[4] just as Ka'b al-Aḥbār was the rabbi (*ḥabr*) of the Arabs. Al-Aswad ibn Yazīd struggled in prayer and fasting, so much so that his body turned green and yellow. When death approached he wept, and when people asked him why he was so sorrowful, he said: "Should I not be sad; who has greater cause to be sad than I? Verily, even were God to forgive me, yet would I weep for shame before him, for all those things I have done." The narrator adds: "He was nothing but a monk among monks."[5] Muwarriaq "stood praying like a *rāhib*." When he was engaged in prayer he was totally unaware of the world. He used to say to his wife: "If you have any messages for me, give them to me now, before I rise to pray."[6] Sometimes the use of a woollen cloak is mentioned, with disapproval, as if it were a custom foreign to Islam. One day Abū 'Aliya was visited by a friend who wore a woollen cloak. Then he said: "Such is the custom of monks. The faithful dress elegantly, when they go to visit one another."[7] Here a *rāhib* is contrasted with one of the faithful. *Rāhib*, we conclude, means primarily the Christian monk and hermit, and when one of the faithful is called by this term, whether as an expression of praise or disapproval, it always signifies a conscious comparison with a phenomenon foreign to Islam. An examination of the whole of that rich material found in the ten volumes of Abū Nu'aym's collection of hagiographies, *Ḥilyat al-auliyā'*, shows that *rāhib* is used only in exceptional cases as a general descriptive term for an ascetic. Dhū'n-Nūn speaks of the perfect saints who ask God for forgiveness before they have sinned, and who receive their reward before they have carried out the works of obedience: "They are the most devout of monks, kings among the servants of God, rulers among the ascetics, because of that plentiful rain which streams down into their hearts, when they, on their way to God, thirst, longing for Him."[8] When, on the other hand, a pious young girl who is pining away with longing for her heavenly Friend, and who is therefore advised by her relatives to see a doctor, calls Aḥmad ibn Abī'l-Ḥawārī "the ascetic (*rāhib*) who is a physician,"[9] the narrator's aim is evidently rather to suggest that she, as a woman, is using a layman's form of words.

One may therefore take it for granted that whenever a reference is made in Arabic ascetic texts to conversations between one of the faithful and a *rāhib*, the latter term indicates a Christian ascetic. One can be fully certain in every case where an ascetic is found in a church, a monastery or a hermit's cell. Muslim ascetics did not as a rule occupy separate cells like the Christian hermits. "The monastic cell of the faithful one," it is written, "is his house, where he keeps his tongue and his eye and his desire under control."[10] In accordance with this rule, during the earliest period of Islam certain ascetics arranged for a cell or subterranean chamber to be built in or under their own houses, where, periodically, they practiced a life of quasi-eremitism. Besides, the conversations which are reported never allude to the teachings of Islam, quotations from the Qur'an or similar matters. As a rule it is the Muslim who gains spiritual instruction from the monk, and the wisdom the latter can offer consists of certain general truths concerning the inner life and the road to God. I choose one example taken from an ascetic in the second century: "I met a *rāhib* once and asked him: 'Do you never fear solitude?'

He replied: 'If you had tasted the delight of solitude, you would long for it, away from your self. Solitude is the beginning of the worship of God.'

'What is the first thing you find in solitude?'

'Peace far from human intercourse and safety far from those evils which accompany it.'

'When may the servant taste the bliss of intimacy with God?'

'When his love for God becomes pure and he communes with him with a sincere heart.'

'When is his love pure?'

'When all his desires are concentrated in one: to obey God.'"[11]

Another pious man once met a monk "in a church in Syria" and received the following counsel: "The most immediate concern for those who love is that of reaching the goal of their desires, and the deepest concern of those who fear is that of escaping from fear and finding security. The one as well as the other is on a good road. But the former is more steadfast and has reached a higher rank of that which is good."[12]

In matters of faith and ritual duties, a Muslim finds sufficient guidance in the holy book and holy tradition of Islam. But in order to learn the method and the ways of ascetic life the teaching of monks may well be useful. Mālik ibn Dīnār, who—as we have noted—was himself called the *rāhib* of the Arabs, does not scorn learning from the Christian monks: "Once, on a mountain, I saw a monk and I asked him: 'Teach me something which can lead me to abandon the world.'

'Are you not a man who has Qur'an and *furqān*?'

'Yes, but I wish you to teach me something which can make me abandon the world.'

'If you are capable of erecting an iron wall between yourself and your desires, then do so."[13]

The conversations contain nothing which could not have been spoken by a Muslim ascetic, either, and in many cases the meeting with the monk is probably a piece of fiction. Islam's devotional writers very often use a particular literary form in order to add interest to their admonitions and maxims, just as our preachers and clergy use the pious anecdote, the factual truth of which is of no great concern either to the speaker or to his listeners. The man of the East has a particular taste for that which is romantic, intriguing and colorful. For instance, the pious man wandering in the desert wilds, in the dark of night or in storm and rain encounters a solitary, young and defenceless girl; out of a ruin there crawls an old man, whose eyebrows hang down over his eyes and whose skin resembles a worn out leather bag; among the crowds of the great city he comes across a black slave, who is said to be mad and acts like a madman; and these people are used as mouthpieces for those edifying thoughts the author wants to convey. The Christian hermit has probably also been seen as a mysterious and picturesque figure, well suited to making an appearance in such a context.

But the conversations do not always recapitulate pious commonplaces from the storehouse of Muslim asceticism itself. Often the monk has something to teach, which, even though distorted and misunderstood, carries a clear Christian imprint. A pious man meets a hermit who looks down at him from his cell on the slope of a hill. He asks the hermit why he keeps himself shut in like this, and receives the answer: "In our holy scriptures we read that Adam's body was created from dust and his spirit from the kingdom of heaven. When you force the body to endure hunger, wakefulness, and nakedness, the spirit longs for its home, the place from whence it came. But when you allow the body to eat, drink or sleep, the body forms an attachment to the place from which it came and knows of no better place than the world."[14] This is the *leitmotif* of Christian monastic asceticism, albeit in an unrefined form: the spirit, imprisoned in the body, gains its freedom to the extent that the body is weakened. Such conversations between Muslims and Christian monks obviously are not without a basis in reality. In any case they bear witness to the fact that Islam, during the first centuries, dared to learn, and in fact did learn, from Christian ascetic piety.

Muslim seekers noticed at an early stage how the Christians venerated the heroes and virtuosi of the ascetic life. The holy man is a precious possession of the community or tribe, honored according to his worth and guarded with jealousy. These things made an impression on pious men within Islam, too, and attracted them to follow the narrow path of rejecting the world. No lesser man than Ibrāhīm ibn Adham, the foremost apostle and saint of early Sufism, tells candidly how he first learned the way from a holy monk: "I learned the knowledge of God from a monk, whose name was Abba Simeon. I went to see him in his cell and asked him: 'Abba Simeon, how long have you lived in this cell of yours?'

He replied: 'For seventy years.'

'And what do you eat?'

'O *ḥanīf*, what makes you ask that?'

'I should very much like to know.'

'Well, then, one pea every night.'

'And what is it that fortifies your soul so that you can satisfy your hunger with one single pea?'

'Do you see the monastery down there, in front of you? Once every year the monks come to me, decorate my cell, walk around it in procession and honour me. Every time my soul becomes lethargic and slow in its devotions I recall that occasion. And thus I gain strength to endure one year of effort for that one moment of glory. You too must seek to endure a moment of effort for eternal glory.' Thus he poured into my heart reverence for divine knowledge. Finally he said: 'Have you received enough, or do you ask for even more?'

'I desire more.' Then he gave me a wineskin containing twenty peas and told me: 'God down to the monastery. They have seen what I have given you.'

I went and when I had entered the monastery, the Christians gathered around me and said: 'O *ḥanīf*, what has the sheikh given to you?'

'Some of his food.'

'What are you going to do with that? We have a greater right to it than you do. State your price!'

'Twenty dinars.'

And so they paid me twenty dinars, whereupon I returned to the old man, who asked: 'What have you done with the peas?'

'I sold them.'

'For how much?'

'For twenty dinars.'

'You were wrong to do that. If you had asked twenty thousand, they would have paid you that. Lo, such great glory has a man who does not serve Him. Imagine then the glory that must belong to him who truly serves God. Turn, O *ḥanīf*, completely towards your Lord and abandon this coming and going."

Abba Simeon's last words suggest that secretly he is a Muslim and looks down on his Christian followers as being in error. The pious narrator has felt himself obliged to describe the matter in this way, in order to explain how a faithful Muslim was able to gain knowledge and inspiration from a Christian. At an earlier stage one would not have found such caution to be necessary. The teachings of the Qur'an made it possible, in principle, to show the very greatest tolerance towards foreign religious communities in all cases where these were people of a Book. All those who faithfully follow their prophet, whether he be called Jesus, Moses or Muhammad, are true worshipers of God, according to the Qur'an. Those particular ritual commandments which each community is to keep and which may differ from one another do not concern essentials. Judaism, Christianity and Islam should thus, in principle, be one. But the Muslim attitude to Jews and Christians is, in fact, different. Even the Qur'an itself teaches that most Christians and Jews have not been faithful to the revelation which they have received, but they have changed and falsified it.

That spiritual affinity which was felt by the ascetics of Islam for the Christian hermits, and the actual correspondence between the life and teachings of the two groups was given a tentative explanation by pious

Muslims; the Christian hermits are in fact a remnant of Jesus' original community, who have kept the true faith pure and authentic and therefore find themselves in full agreement with the teachings of the holy book of Islam. According to the Sufi writer al-Tirmidhī, Ibn 'Abbās taught that eremitism arose when, after the death of Jesus, tyrannical kings falsified the Gospels and the Torah. Some dedicated Christians then opposed their willful action and explained: "He who does not keep to that which God has revealed is an infidel." When Abū Bakr sent his armies to Syria, he is said to have given the following order often: "You will find people who have shut themselves up in cells. Leave them alone; it is for the sake of God they have shut themselves in. You will also find others, whom Satan has branded on the tops of their heads. Cut their heads off, wherever you find them."[16] The monks with their tonsures, those ascetics who have not had the patience to endure in solitude but have escaped from their cells into the monasteries, in so doing have proved themselves to be children of the Devil. To them one should show no mercy.

That the hermits (or at least some of them) are Christians of the original, and true, confession, that which is in agreement with Islam, and that they have taken refuge in their desert cells in order not to have to accept the detestable doctrine that God has a Son, is also the view of Khālid ibn Yazīd, an ascetic from the first century AH. He relates a dramatic encounter with such hermits and their leader. They live in an inaccessible wilderness area in Jazīra, in a somewhat similar manner to Swedenborg's spiritually enlightened Negroes in the heart of Africa.[17] Fantastic legends are told about these true disciples of Christ. "The dwelling of the people of 'Ad" is an imaginary city somewhere in the vast unknown lands of central Arabia and it is a kind of *Blocksberg* for holy persons, to whichever faith they may belong.[18] That is where, according to the legend, Sahl ibn 'Abdallāh met "one of Christ's disciples. He wore a woollen mantle which seemed brand new, but he told me: 'I have worn this mantle since the days of Christ.' When I marvelled at this, he said: 'It is not the body which wears out clothes, but the stench of sins and forbidden food."[19]

Generally speaking, during the Omayyad era there existed an attitude not only of tolerance, but in many areas, and especially in ascetic circles, even an attitude of benevolence, towards the Christians. Still in the case of Muḥammad ibn Yūsuf al-Isbahānī, who died in 184 AH (-800 AD), it is told that when he saw a Christian, he would honor him and give him presents in order to win him over to Islam. Not a few pious Muslims considered it permissible to greet their Christian friends with the greeting of peace, *salām*, otherwise reserved for the faithful. A man met his eye doctor, who was a Christian, and accidentally happened to greet him with a *salām*. He sought the advice of an-Nakhā'ī (d. 95 AH, 715 AD), who declared without hesitation: "There is nothing wrong in your saying *salām* to him, if you have business with him or if there is friendship between you."[20] Such lack of prejudice afterwards caused astonishment and has puzzled later hagiographers considerably. In their opinion he cannot really have been talking about *salām*, but about some more general greeting: "How are you?" or something similar.[21]

Recognition and approval from the side of Christian authorities is valued very highly. On one occasion, when Sufyān ath-Thaurī was ill, his nephew took a sample of his urine to the head of a Christian monastery, who was a knowledgeable physician. He expressed his opinion: "This cannot be the urine of a *ḥanīf*"—*ḥanīf* being the title which the monks were in the habit of using when speaking of their Muslim counterparts. The expression suggests the dogmatic presupposition for spiritual fellowship between Christians and Muslims: a *ḥanīf* being a follower of the true, prophetic, original religion whose adherents, despite differences in outward forms, are united in faith. The head of the monastery went to see the sick man, felt his stomach and examined his perspiration, and then gave his opinion: "I did not believe that such things existed among the *ḥanīf*s; this is a man, whose liver has been consumed by sorrow."[22] This was, in a way, a high mark from the most competent of judges. It was also considered an honor if Christian monks called a pious ascetic a "friend of Jesus."

The sense of spiritual affinity with Christianity, or rather with that form of Christianity which was regarded as original and orthodox, is also expressed in the dominant position Jesus occupies in the pronouncements and ideas of the ascetics. The prophets most often named and quoted in pious legends and sayings (as a rule free inventions) are Jesus, Moses, David and John the Baptist, in that order. Jesus is, without comparison, placed first among the four. One might say, without exaggeration, that on the deepest level of ascetic piety he is of far greater importance than Islam's own prophet, if, that is, one were able to disregard Muhammad's position as the original source and guarantor of *Sunna*, the highly revered and strictly followed tradition. The ascetics of the earliest period are in fact generally the most faithful adherents of the *Sunna*. However, the process of selection and editing carried out by later hagiographers was to remove every trace of an earlier and more liberal attitude.

Knowledge of the life and work of Jesus was extended considerably during the first centuries, from those unclear and [apparently] apocryphal items of information given in the Qur'an. Among the features in his life which are known to the ascetic tradition, the following are new to Islam:the story of the wise men, the flight into Egypt, Jesus settles in Nazareth, the temptation in the desert, Jesus calls his disciples, Jesus walks on the water, the raising of Lazarus, the cleansing of the Temple and, as we we shall see below, the Passion, ascension and resurrection of Jesus.

Clearly, the earliest ascetics in Islam possessed, or at any rate may have possessed, a not inconsiderable knowledge of the figure of Jesus as he is shown in the Gospels. It is striking, however, how comparatively insignificant a part these features played in the formation of that image of Jesus which really lived in the faith of pious Muslims. The Muslim Christ is above all the great ascetic, the ideal image of the saint who, liberated from all earthly needs and bonds, wanders about and sleeps out in the open, with a stone for a pillow. Like the *bhikku* he carries no money; but in contrast to the Buddhist monk, who still has his sieve and his begging bowl, he carries no tools or possessions of any kind, nor does he beg for his food. He takes what nature offers him: the water in the spring and the plants growing in the soil. In a popular tradition[23] it is written: Jesus never saved anything from his evening meal for the morning, or from his morning meal for the evening. He ate of the leaves of the trees and drank rainwater, dressed in sackcloth or garments made of hair, and spent the night wherever he happened to be when darkness fell. He said: "Every day has its sustenance ordained by God." According to Ka'b al-Aḥbār "he wore his hair long and never anointed his head." "He went barefoot, owned no house, used no ornaments, household goods, fine clothes or coins, and only carried food for one day. Wherever he found himself at sunset, there he remained standing in prayer until dawn." Thus he exercised the utmost degree of renunciation of the world. At the outset he carried a comb and a waterskin. But one day he saw a man combing his hair with his fingers. Then he laid his comb aside. On another occasion he saw a man drinking water straight from a brook, whereupon he put away even his waterskin.[24] Overall, Jesus is the ideal ascetic and mystic. "The disciples asked Jesus: 'Is there anyone on earth who is like you?' He answered: 'Yes, he whose words are a reflection upon God, whose silence is meditation and the sight of whom is an exhortation to souls.'"[25] Incidentally, these same writers also knew fairly well what Jesus looked like. He was a "a man of medium height, ruddy-complexioned though slightly pale, who wore his hair straight and inclined his head to one side."[26] At the end of the second century AH a man named Abū Dharḥa is mentioned as the one who, of all people, most closely resembled Jesus, the son of Mary.[27] Unfortunately we do not know what Abū Dharḥa looked like, but presumably he would have resembled that wonderful portrait of Christ which King Abgar owned, according to the Acts of Thaddaeus, and which is said to have been the basis of numerous descriptions of the actual appearance of Christ.

Ascetic piety might simply be called "following the way of Christ." In a tradition expressed in the laboriously solemn and oracular style of Shi'ite propaganda. Nauf al-Kalbī narrates: "I saw 'Alī step outside one evening and look at the stars. Thereupon he said: 'Do you sleep, Nauf, or are you looking attentively?'

'I am looking, O ruler of the faithful.'

'O Nauf, blessed are those who renounce this world and long for the next. It is such people who use the earth as their sleeping-mat, its dust as their resting-place, its water as their perfume and the Qur'an and prayer as their mantle and clothing. They bid the world follow the way of Christ."[28]

In the Muslim image of Jesus we find other traits having a clear inner affinity with the Gospels, even though they have not been taken directly from the New Testament tradition. Jesus is foremost among ascetics, yet he is different from all other ascetics. Although strict with himself, he is full of compassion towards others. Mālik ibn Dīnār repeats a saying, supposedly of Jesus himself: "Do not look upon the sins of men, as though you were their Lord, but look on them as one who is himself a servant. There are two kinds of people: those who are struck down (by suffering and sin) and those who are sound and healthy. Be merciful towards the suffering and thank God for those who are well."[29] The fact that Jesus recognizes the good even in those despised and rejected by others, finds symbolic expression in a well-known story, also originating from Mālik ibn Dīnār: "Jesus and his disciples walked past a dead dog. The disciples said: 'How disgustingly he stinks!' But Jesus said: 'How white his teeth are!' In this manner he exhorted them not to speak ill of anyone."[30]

Above all Jesus is compassionate toward sinners. "Once he was seen leaving the house of a harlot, and people said to him: 'O, Spirit of God, what are you doing in the house of such a woman?' But he answered: 'The physician must visit the sick."[31] For the sinner who repents and amends his life is, in the eyes of God, just as good as the righteous man who is proud and arrogant. The reward of humility and the dangers of spiritual arrogance are described in an imaginative Arabic variation on the theme of the Pharisee and the tax-collector: "Jesus and one of his disciples once passed a robber, who was lying in wait in his mountain hideaway. When the robber saw them, God prompted him to amend his life. He thought: 'Now here is Jesus, the son of Mary, God's Spirit and

His Word, and here is this disciple of his. But what about you, you wretch? You are a robber among the children of Israel. You have lain in ambush by the roadside, you have taken people's possessions and shed their blood.' Thereupon he descended from the mountain, filled with remorse over his former life. Having caught up with Jesus and the disciple, he said to himself: 'You want to walk together with them! You are not worthy to walk alongside them. Walk behind them. Walk as befits an evildoer and a sinner!' Now when the disciple turned around and recognized the robber, he thought: 'Look at this wretched villain walking behind us!' But God saw the thoughts of their hearts: in the one remorse and repentance, and in the other pride and scorn, and he sent a revelation to Jesus: 'Tell the disciple and the robber that both of them will be allowed to begin their work of piety as from the beginning. For I have forgiven the robber all his former crimes, because he repented and did penance. And all the previous acts of piety of the disciple have lost their value, because he was full of pride and despised the penitent robber.'"[32]

For Jesus, humility is the supreme virtue. "He said to the children of Israel: 'Where does the grain grow?'

'In the dust.'

'Verily I say unto you: Wisdom can only grow in a heart that has become like the dust.'"[33] Before you exhort others, you must examine your own heart: "God revealed this to Jesus: First exhort yourself, and when you have taken the exhortation to heart, then you may also exhort others. If you act in the opposite way, you should feel ashamed before me."[34] Jesus, like other imperfect human beings, thus needs to examine himself. In certain ascetic circles the doctrine of Christ's sinlessness had been adopted at an early stage. Jesus was free from certain earthly desires, simply due to his supernatural birth. Thus he felt no desire for women, since he had not been conceived from human seed.[35] Otherwise there is no direct relationship between his sinlessness and supernatural conception. It was through a special dispensation of God that both Jesus and Mary had been preserved from the taint of sin. According to Abū Hurayra, the Prophet said: "Satan touches every child that is born, and when he touches it, the child raises its voice and cries. This is what has happened to every child except Mary and Jesus. Read the Word of God: I shall protect her and her offspring against every spirit of evil." Qatāda said that Satan drives a spear into the side of every newborn infant. But when Mary and Jesus were born, God placed a curtain before them. The point of the Devil's spear hit the curtain and did not reach the child.[36]

Jesus did not return evil for evil, nor did he repay taunts and hard words in the same coin. "Jesus, the son of Mary, once walked past some people who were jeering at him. He continued on his way and met others who also mocked him. But every time he was met by evil words, he answered with good words. Then one of his disciples said: 'The more evil people speak to you, the more you reply with good. It seems as though you yourself wanted to excite people against you and encourage them to taunt you.' But Jesus answered: 'A person gives to others that which he or she carries within.'"[37] The story reinforces the maxim: "Bless those who curse you," and at the same time alludes to another Gospel saying: "A good man produces good from the store of good within himself; and an evil man from evil within produces evil." (LK 6:45)

Jesus was as strict in his ascetic practices as was John the Baptist. But in contrast to John, who was rough and gloomily serious, Jesus was joyful, kind, and outgoing. Jesus and John met, and Jesus smiled at John and stretched out his hand to him. Then John said: "My cousin, why do I see you smile, as if you already felt safe from God's punishment?' Jesus answered: 'And why do I see you frown as if you already despaired of salvation?' Then God revealed himself to both of them: 'The one of you who is dearer to me, is the one who is more joyful and kind to his neighbour.'"[38]

Words and sayings of Jesus occur very frequently in Islamic devotional literature. In many cases these sayings, though ascribed to Jesus, show no traces of New Testament or even Christian provenance. They reflect the religious thought of Islam and use its theological vocabulary. But there are not infrequent exceptions to the rule.

The New Testament material has apparently penetrated into Islam by way of oral tradition. When Muhammad received his earliest revelations he was certainly not literate. He states expressly: "Not before this (the Qur'an) didst thou recite any Book, or inscribe it with the right hand" (Sura 29:47). The term 'Book' signifies any written document, be it book or letter. Thus the Prophet could neither read nor write. To the Prophet himself, as to faithful Muslims to this day, this is conclusive proof of the divine origin of the Qur'an. When a man who is completely illiterate brings forth a scripture unsurpassed in clarity, beauty, and eloquence, it cannot stem from the man himself. It must have come from God. To imagine that Muhammad was claiming to be more ignorant than he really was—as confessional or rationalist polemicists have occasionally tried to suggest—is unacceptable to the modern study of religion, which possesses greater knowledge of the psychological nature and the conditions of inspiration. Muhammad himself must have been wholly convinced that that which he recited was God's own word, and that it had come to him without his own person being in any way involved. Otherwise it would be impossible to explain how he could have given others the same absolute certainty. As H.S. Nyberg has pointed out,

Muhammad was familiar with *gematria*, the letter magic which flourished in the semi-Christian sects of his day, and he must have known the letters.[39] It is very likely that he gradually gained a certain degree of literacy. His opponents note in a later Sura from Medina: "This is naught . . . but fairy-tales of the ancients that he has had written down, so that they are recited to him at the dawn and in the evening" (Sura 25:5–6). From this it appears that Muhammad, in the opinion of his opponents, is now literate, and he himself does not dispute their point in this respect. On the other hand he can defend himself with a good conscience against their accusations. His ability to read did not, however, extend to the biblical scriptures, which he knew only in non-Arabic language. Nor did he write down dictated translations. This was not the way it happened. That which he learnt in conversations with Christians and Jews was taken up by his creative imagination and reproduced more or less freely. His book is truly his spiritual testimony.

The situation was hardly different for Muhammad's first disciples. Their ability to read and write was considerably greater, but the biblical writings appear to have been largely a closed world to them. And for those who had, or may have had, some knowledge (for instance new converts who had grown up in a Christian or Jewish environment), it was always a hazardous undertaking to quote biblical texts literally, since one might so easily come into conflict with Qur'anic statements concerning the Torah and the Gospels. That which could be transmitted concerning the scriptures of "the peoples of the Book" was in any case based mainly on oral information, and where such information was not available one turned to the pious imagination and used it even more freely than did Muhammad himself. There were also the popular story-tellers (*quṣṣāṣ*), those who used to gather crowds of eager listeners in the mosques, who had made the legends of the Prophet and the biblical stories their speciality. It should however be said, to do them justice, that in former times they strove not only to entertain but above all to edify by their touching and fascinating pious tales, just as popular preachers still do today.

One of the foremost first-generation Muslim experts on biblical matters was Ka'b al-Aḥbār, who died during the caliphate of 'Uthmān. Clearly, that which he had to pass on came largely out of his own storehouse. A lengthy dialogue between God and Abraham, a no less detailed summary of Moses' conversation with God on the holy mountain and other similar narratives are apparently pure fiction, composed in the manner of the pious storytellers and probably never meant to reproduce reality in the historical sense. Also, they are purely Muslim in form and content, even though occasional features here and there testify to some familiarity with Christian apocrypha. For instance, when Gabriel addresses Adam as Holy Spirit, one is inevitably reminded of some Gnostic Adamic scripture. A large part of his material consists of legends: about Abraham and the Angel of Death, the grave of Joseph, Gog and Magog, the Guardians of Hell and similar stories.[40] One legend tells, for example, how Jesus finds a human skull and, with God's permission, raises the dead man. The latter immediately finds himself in the very place where he left his earthly life: on his way to market with a bundle of vegetables, and he cannot at all grasp that he has been dead. The legends *may* of course have been taken from late Christian apocrypha or from Jewish *Haggada*—the whole of this material deserves investigation from the point of view of *Märchengeschichte.*

However, among the *Israelitica* of Ka'b one also finds—albeit more sparingly—genuine biblical reminiscences. "Two men came to the door of the mosque. One went in. The other one did not enter, but said: 'A man like myself is not worthy to enter into the house of my Lord.' Then God appeared before one of the prophets of Israel: 'Lo, I have made him righteous, because he thus abased himself.'"[42] The parable of the Pharisee and the tax-collector is retold here, Ka'b apparently being unaware of the fact that it stems from Jesus. With the same or even greater liberty another Gospel saying is rendered: "Moses has said: 'You dress in the robes of monks, but your hearts are the hearts of evildoers and howling wolves. If you desire the kingdom of heaven, then kill your hearts for the sake of God."[43] The saying from Matthew 7:15 is attributed to Moses. As a rule Ka'b never acknowledges the Gospels or Jesus himself as the source of his biblical quotations. This is perhaps unintentional, however. The older ascetic literature often drew no clear distinction between Torah and the Gospels. As a prophet of Israel Jesus is also supposed to have figured in the revealed Jewish record. It is probably not fortuitous, on the other hand, that several of the Jewish sayings quoted by Ka'b are found both in the Old and the New Testaments. A saying from Isaiah concerning the servant of the Lord is quoted as a prophecy about Muhammad in the Torah: "Muhammad is My servant, the trusted one, the chosen one. He is not hard or coarse, he will not shout in the marketplaces. He does not return evil for evil but is lenient and forgiving."[44] The source may be Isa. 42:1–2 or Matt. 12:18. The following saying, which may come from Micah 7:6 or Matthew 10:35, is said to be "written in the Torah": "The worst enemies of a pious man are his own family, and those closest to him are his opponents."[45] Traces of both the New and the Old Testaments are found in an eschatological saying concerning how "Constantinople rejoiced over the destruction of Jerusalem and grew powerful and haughty, and came to be called 'the proud and arrogant one'. And she said: 'If the throne of God is founded on the seas, the seas themselves have their foundations in me.' But God promised to punish her even before the Day of Judgment. He asked: 'Verily, I shall remove your jewels and your silk and leave you deserted, so that no man will ever raise a cry within you. No one shall stand on your walls, no one live in you except jackals. Nothing will grow in you except stones and prickly bushes, and I shall leave nothing between you and the heavens. Three kinds of fire I shall let fall upon you: the fire of pitch, the fire of tar and the fire of naptha. And I shall leave you mutilated and bald, and your cry will be heard even unto heaven."[46] Here the main source was *Revelation*, chapters 17 and 18—this is evident from the very fact that the prophecy is applied to Byzantium (Rome). Certain details may however have been borrowed from the Old Testament (Isa. 13:22, Jer. 50:39). Over and above these hints there is found only one clear allusion to the Old Testament: "God says: 'The sons shall repay the sins of their fathers. I shall punish the one who disobeys Me, generation after generation unto the third. And I shall keep the one who has obeyed Me, generation after generation unto the tenth"[47] (cf. Deut. 5:9–10).

To complete the picture of Ka'b the Scribe it should finally be pointed out that in the interests of orthodoxy he could also permit himself pure and evident falsification. According to Ka'b, the Torah ends with the following words: "Praise be to God, who has no Son and no partner in his kingdom"—and this is a direct quotation from the Qur'an.

In Muslim tradition Ka'b is said to have been "one of the great scholars among the peoples of the Book,"[48] who converted to Islam during the caliphate of Abū Bakr. Thus one cannot know if he was originally a Jew or a Christian, and his own statements provide no clear distinction between the Torah and the Gospels. Such a position would undoubtedly have been easier for a Christian, who knew and used both the Old and New Testaments, than for a Jew. The fact that Ka'b originated from Himyar in South Arabia may also be taken as evidence pointing to Christianity. However, we cannot estimate his scriptural knowledge as highly as did those later Muslim writers. One might have been able to expect the occasional correct quotation from some biblical scripture by a man who had himself read the holy books. To judge from the evidence, he was an unlettered man, who drew from the supply of popular legends and freely rendered biblical sayings he had come to know in the oral tradition within which he had grown up.

Alongside Ka'b as an authority concerning the religious traditions and holy scriptures of the peoples of the book, there stands another Yemeni, Wahb ibn Munabhih, who lived one generation later (he died in AH 114–732 AD). Wahb's learning is on quite a different level from that of Ka'b. This learning is demonstrated in two works: *Mubtadā* and *Isrāʾīliyyāt*, which have now been lost, but large parts of which have been preserved in a work by Muḥammad ibn Ibrāhīm al-Tha'labī (died AH 427–1036–7 AD), entitled *'Arā'is al-bayān* for which they formed one of the main sources. As we shall see, he was extremely well informed about Christianity. Allusions to Old Testament texts also occur, although less frequently. These he reproduced with an evident lack of concern, either in respect of form or attribution of authorship. I quote a couple of examples: "Some Israelites asked their prophet about the Lord, where He was to be found, and in which house He lived, and asked: 'Should we build a house for him and worship him there?' Then God sent this reply to the prophet: 'Your people ask Me where I may be found, that they may worship Me, and which house contains Me. The heavens and the earth cannot contain Me. But when they ask where I live, I will answer them: Lo, I live in an abstemious, peaceable and pious heart'" (cf. Isa. 66:1–2).[49] "David says: 'Woe unto an age when one seeks to gather the pious ones and can find none, save as one finds an ear of corn where the reapers have been, or a cluster of grapes where the pickers pass through" (cf. Isa. 17:56).[50] In Wahb, too, one encounters "scriptural sayings" which are clearly Muslim in content and style but are apparently independent inventions. Such creative license is however not to be regarded as falsification in our sense of the word. The words "God says in the Torah" or "I read in one of the Scriptures of the peoples of the Book" have become a formula, by which one may simply and without scruple introduce sayings which have been found to be especially edifying, or the truth of which has been seen as immutably certain. The quotations from the biblical apocrypha are thus used in the same way as the so-called *ḥadīth qudsī*, a saying which is introduced by the words "God says," without the intention of asserting that those words are in fact to be found in any revealed scripture.

The matter certainly takes on a different complexion when the source is quoted more precisely: "I have read thirty lines at the end of the Psalms" or "four consecutive lines in the Torah," and when sayings quoted have no connection whatever with the Old Testament. Nor is Wahb always completely *bona fide* when he lends his supposed biblical learning to the service of Muslim apologetics. "I have read," he writes, "ninety or so of God's revealed scriptures; seventy or more that are well known among the learned, and twenty which only a few people know, and in all of them it is written that whosoever ascribes to himself any free will is an infidel."[51] Wahb had every reason to demonstrate his orthodoxy by bringing forth this powerful argument against the heretical belief in the freedom of the will. He was in fact suspected of having been a *qadarite* for a time, thus having fallen himself into the very same heresy. All in all, he had a very high opinion of his own learning and quotes a most comprehensive body of literature, which he himself claims to have studied. The titles of the books are not given, but it is obvious that he is thinking not only of revelatory scriptures in the proper sense, whether canonical or apocryphal, but of religious and edifying writings in general. As far as can be ascertained, his sources were Christian and, if they were in fact written sources, they apparently included several Christian monastic texts. Palladius tells how Satan attempts to seduce a monk to spiritual pride by showing himself to him in the form of Christ. Whoever has been graced by a vision of Christ is therefore perfectly 'spiritual' (*pneumatikós*), and no longer subject to the discipline and order that applies to ordinary monks.[51] It is told of one of the Fathers that "when he was sitting in his cell, pressing towards the spiritual goal, the demons appeared to him, face to face, and sought to disturb him, but he rejected them with contempt. When Satan found himself vanquished in this way by the pious man, he appeared before him in human guise and said: 'I am Christ.' When the old man saw him, he only winked at him and mocked him. Then Satan said: 'Yes, I myself am Christ.' The old man replied: 'I do not wish to see Christ here.' When Satan heard this, he left him."[52] Wahb tells the same legend: "In the days of the Messiah a monk lived alone in his cell. The devil wished to deceive him, but was unable to do so, despite constant attempts. Then he came to him in the form of Christ and said: 'Monk, arise, I want to talk to you.' But the monk said: 'Mind your own business. I cannot add anything to that period of my life which has passed.' Satan, however, went on: 'Stand up while I am talking to you; I am Christ.'

'Even if you are Christ, what have I to do with you? Did you not, once and for all, command us to serve God and proclaim to us the message of the resurrection? Go away, I have no need of you.' And the devil left him instantly and went away."[54]

Another story told by Wahb concerns a monk, who had learned that the king of that country intended to visit him. He sat down with a large bowl of vegetables, oil and peas, ate voraciously and pretended not to notice his visitor. The king thought that anyone eating with such an appetite could not possibly be a holy man, and went away, disappointed. But the monk praised God that he had been able to make the king despise him.[55] The same legend is told by Palladius about Abba Simeon.[56]

As an example of Wahb's knowledge of the contents of the New Testament we may note his description of the suffering, death and resurrection of Jesus. This is a very sensitive subject. The Qur'an expressly disputes the fact that Jesus died on the cross and therefore does not acknowledge his resurrection. Jesus was taken up to heaven directly, the Jews having been struck by God himself with blindness, and thus having crucified a substitute in his place. Despite this, Wahb is prepared to acknowledge that Jesus really died: "When God gave Jesus to understand that he was to leave the world, he was deeply saddened and was filled with deep sorrow. He gathered his disciples around him, prepared a meal for them and gave them this message: 'Come to me this evening, I have something to say to you.' When they had gathered in his house and night fell, he stood up and served them. And when they had finished eating, he washed their hands, gave them a farewell message and then dried their hands with his clothing. They found this too great a thing and disapproved of his doing it. But he said: 'Whoever disapproves of what I do, he is not in me and I am not in him.' Then they allowed him to continue. Thereupon he said to them: 'That which I have done unto you this night, when I have served you at table and washed your hands with my own hand, this has been done as an example to you. You believe that I am the first among you. Therefore, may no one among you consider himself greater than another. And may every one among you give himself for the other, as I have given myself for you. But in one matter I now ask for your help: you will pray to God for me and entreat him to delay my passing.' Now when they rose to pray and desired to continue in prayer, God covered them with sleep, so that they were not able to pray. Then Jesus roused them, saying: 'Can you not persevere in helping me this one night?' They replied: 'In God's name, we do not know what is the matter with us. Usually we are quite able to watch, but tonight we cannot do it, and as soon as we try to pray, something intervenes to prevent us.' He said: 'The shepherd goes away, and the sheep are left.' And he also spoke other words with a similar meaning, alluding to himself. Then he said: 'One of you will betray me, before the cock has crowed three times. And one of you will sell me for a small sum of money and throw away the payment he has received for me.' Then they went out and parted. But the Jews were searching for Jesus. That is when they caught Simon, one of the disciples, and said: 'This is one of this disciples.' But he denied it, saying: 'I am not among his followers.' They left him in peace. Later another one caught him and he made the same denial. Then he heard the sound of the cock-crow, and wept with sorrow. When morning came, one of the disciples went to the Jews and asked: 'What will you give me, if I show you where to find him?' Then they gave him thirty *dirham*. And he showed them the way to Jesus. Before that, they had not known with certainty who he was. Now they took Jesus, bound him with a rope and took him to the place of execution, saying: 'You have awakened the dead and made the blind to see. Will you not free yourself from this rope, then?'

And they spat on him, and threw thorns at him. Thereupon they erected a cross to crucify him. But when they brought him to the cross, darkness fell over the earth. And God sent angels, who separated Jesus from his tormentors and placed the bodily form of Jesus upon the one who had directed them to him. His name was Judas. They crucified him instead, believing that he was Jesus. But Jesus died and remained dead for three hours. Thereupon God raised him to heaven and he remained in heaven for seven days. Then God said: 'Your enemies prevented you from completing the pact with your disciples. Descend to them, therefore, and give them a farewell exhortation. Descend also to Mary Magdalene, for no one has wept and mourned for you as she has done. Tell her that she shall be the first to follow you and that she shall gather your disciples, that they may travel through the whole world and call people to God. . . .' At God's command Jesus thus descended, seven days after his glorification, to Mary Magdalene and the mountain blazed with light when he descended. Mary now gathered his disciples around him and he sent them out to call people to God. Thereupon God elevated him to heaven and clothed him in light and freed him from any desire for food and drink. He is now soaring with the angels around the throne of God, a being at one and the same time man and angel, at one and the same time earthly and heavenly. And the night on which he descended is the night which Christians keep as a feast day (Easter)."[57]

We may observe how, from the events at Golgotha and by the empty tomb, Wahb has conveyed, with diplomatic caution, just as much information as can possibly be consistent with the Qur'anic narrative. Otherwise he shows an intimate knowledge of the Christian tradition and a mind filled with ideas and sayings from the Gospels. Has he read the New Testament himself? Despite his own claims as to his incredible erudition this seems hardly likely. If one compares his way of quoting the Qur'an with the manner in which he cites biblical sayings, it is hardly possible to imagine that he has had the text in front of him. Wahb has probably also drawn from oral tradition, reproducing Christian and biblical legends and real or supposed sayings of Jesus and other prophets, which he himself has heard. Such material was not only gathered by the pious storytellers, but was also the object of studies by learned collectors.[58]

It is striking that practically all the New Testament quotations and allusions found in the earlier literature of asceticism come from the Gospels. Of the fifty or so I have noted down, only three are based on the Epistles and one on Revelation; all the others stem from the Gospels. Later Muslim polemicists, for instance Ibn Ḥazm, attacked the apostles bitterly for having falsified the original teachings of Jesus. It seems that writers of the earlier period did not share this attitude, and it is hardly for this reason that they avoid the apostolic letters. It is, however, understandable that the worship of Christ in Paul or John, insofar as it was comprehensible at all, must have appeared both objectionable and senseless. They were, on the other hand, able to understand and absorb the words and sayings of Jesus in the Synoptic Gospels. Many of the sayings in the Gospels hit home by their own force; their incomparable conciseness and concentration also helped to make them common property, even within the religious world of Islam. "Judge not, that ye be not judged," the sayings about the salt of the world, about not throwing pearls before swine, and about the difficulty of a rich man's entering the kingdom of heaven became pious Muslim aphorisms, as anonymous and universally valid as proverbs. It is no coincidence that approximately half of all the New Testament sayings quoted in these sources are found in the Sermon on the Mount.[59]

Thirty or more of these New Testament aphorisms are identified as sayings of Jesus from the Gospels. The others are claimed to be sayings of named Muslims ascetics, of Moses, of Muhammad;[60] or, as coming from the Torah or from "one of the scriptures." Thus the following words are given as a saying by Yaḥyā ibn Abī Kathīr: "Men of learning are like salt, which keeps everything fresh; but when the salt is spoilt, nothing can restore it. It is trodden under foot and thrown away."[61] And Matthew 12:30: "He who is not with me is against me" becomes a saying by Sufyān ath-Thaurī. The narrative of the rich fool (Luke 12:15–21) is quoted as a "story of a man in past times" without any indication of its Gospel source.[62] The episode of Jesus stilling the storm is retold following Mark 4:37–41 very closely, but as a legend concerning Ibrāhīm ibn Adham.[63]

Occasionally the Arabic version reproduces the wording of the Gospels fairly closely. Thus Luke 11:27–28 is quoted in the following words: "Jesus walked past a woman, who said: 'Happy, happy is the womb that carried you, and the breasts that suckled you.' But Jesus said: 'No, happy is the one who reads the Qur'an and keeps that which is written therein.'"[64] But most frequently the biblical words occur in very free paraphrase. I will permit myself a couple of examples: "Jesus said: 'O children of Israel, Moses forbade you to commit adultery, and that was right. But to consider adultery in the heart without committing it is like lighting a fire inside a house of clay. Even if the house does not burn down, at least it is blackened by the smoke. O children of Israel, Moses forbade you to swear by [the name of] God and it is right not to do so. But I forbid you to swear, whether you speak lies or the truth.'"[65] We encounter Jesus' condemnation of the Pharisees, from Matthew 23, in several versions, rendered more or less freely: "God says, in punishing the scribes of Israel: 'You study the law, but not for the sake of faith. You gather knowledge, but not in order to act according to it. By the deeds of the next world you strive to conquer this world. You dress in the skins of sheep and thereby you hide your wolf-like souls. You sieve the insects out of your drinking water, but you swallow mountains of those things which God has forbidden. You make religion weigh upon people like stones; and then refuse to lift a finger to help them. You make your prayers long and your garments white in order to attract the property of widows and orphans. I swear by My omnipotence that I shall send a plague upon you, which will bring to nought the intelligence of the intelligent and the wisdom of the wise.'"[66]

Quite often the link with the biblical text is so tenuous that one is hardly able to discern the prototype. Take, for instance, the following naive description of Jesus' ascetic way of life: "While Jesus was walking in the land of Syria, a violent rainstorm with thunder and lightning came upon him. He therefore looked for a place where he could find shelter. He saw a tent set up in the distance and walked to it. But in the tent he found a woman and at once withdrew from her. Then he discovered a cave, but found that a lion had taken possession of it. He put his hand on the head of the wild beast and said: 'My God, you have given a place of refuge to every living being, it is only for me that you have not provided one.' Then the Glorious One answered: 'Your place of refuge shall be with Me, in the house of My loving-kindness. On the day of resurrection I shall marry you to one hundred houris, whom I have created by My own hand. And at your wedding I shall give a banquet lasting four thousand years. Every day of those four thousand years shall be as long as the whole history of the world; and I shall comand a herald to cry: 'Where are the ascetics of this world? Let them come to the wedding feast of the ascetic, Jesus, the son of Mary.'"[67] The first part of this story is evidently a legend concerning a pious monk's almost intolerable temptations, and also contains an allusion to the oft-quoted saying about Jesus having no home (Matt. 8:20). The latter part, on the other hand, evidently reproduces what a Muslim ascetic had heard and understood of the saying concerning the wedding of the Lamb (Rev. 17:7–9). It is possible, but not certain, that New Testament allusions are to be found in the following words of Sahl: "He, for whom the path is narrow in this world, to him it shall be wide in the next. But he for whom the path is wide in this world, to him it shall become narrow in the next."[68] "Son of Adam: Sell this world for the next, and you shall gain both worlds. But do not sell the world to come for this world, for then you will lose both."[69] "Kill your self, that your self may live."[70]

Now, why should the Gospel sayings be reproduced throughout in paraphrased or reworded forms? One can hardly avoid the conclusion that it must have been a case of rendering, not what had been *read*, but what had been *heard*. Words that were heard in conversations with Christians were freely retold, passed on from speaker to speaker probably over many years and became more and more remote in form from their model. Although there was a certain personal reluctance to read the Gospel of the Christians, believed by orthodox Muslims to be a falsified and dangerous book, instead there was a living translation. Gospel sayings were passed on from one generation to the next, as a deposit of pious spiritual maxims, and to some extent exercised a hidden influence over modes of faith and thought in the world of Islam, in a manner reminiscent of the unobtrusive and indirect mission of the New Testament in present-day India.

The many spiritual dialogues between Muslims and Christian ascetics, whether in darkened cells or on pious walks in the solitude of the hills, of course also left traces over and above the knowledge of Jesus, the son of Mary, how he lived and what he said. Elsewhere I have shown how much Islam learned during the earliest generations about monastic religious practices, outward forms and characteristic lifestyle, material which I do not propose to recapitulate here.[71] But the knowledge also penetrated to a deeper level, that of the spiritual attitude, the ethos and moral ideals of Christian asceticism. It was above all the teachings of the Sermon on the Mount that Muslims learned to imitate—principally those sayings that warn the faithful against desiring to be noticed for their own piety, and against judging and despising others; and those sayings that stress the duty of unlimited forgiveness. The ascetics of Islam learned to value and practise these Gospel virtues in exactly that form which they were given in the piety of the Christian hermits.

When one submits to such rigorous sacrifices, such an iron discipline, and when one accomplishes such heroic feats in the struggle to suppress all human inclinations and desires, it is unavoidable—for such is human nature, after all—to feel a measure of pride over one's own achievements. And when the ascetic remembers the price he has paid to achieve his own salvation, and how cheaply men of the world have attempted to escape these strict demands, he cannot avoid noticing the vast difference between individual human beings. If God is so severe that the pious man stands condemned for taking a pinch of salt with his crust of bread, how, then, is one to regard the individual who eats what he likes and as much as he likes, every day? One is thus able to measure, purely quantitatively, how much better one is than other people.

But conscience is alive and active even in the ascetic Pharisee, and subconscious spiritual perfectionism creates peculiar defensive attitudes in face of those sins of which conscience is quietly accusing us. If one loves to be admired and praised for one's piety, then this evil inclination is compensated for by excessive timidity and fear of being noticed. One uses the most conspicuous means to avoid becoming conspicuous. One tries to create a bad name for oneself, to avoid acquiring a good one. Although one believes oneself to be better than other people, one tries to appear worse than one really is. Although inwardly convinced that others are inferior in piety and spirituality, one exaggerates the duty of not judging but forgiving—to the extent of refusing to see one's brother's faults, thus carrying forbearance and tolerance to extremes, which is rather questionable, morally speaking. On all these points Islam has faithfully followed the pattern of monastic religion. One might quote numerous examples to show how at least a certain body of knowledge related to the life and sayings of the famous monastic saints must have been a living part of the oral tradition transmitted to Muslim ascetics from Christian sources.

That mystical ascetic piety within the Christian churches which had given Muhammad his religious conversion thus continued to exercise considerable influence on the community he founded. This is hardly unexpected, of course. To a great extent Islam adopted the culture of the Christian Mediterranean world, and it is not possible to imagine that its religious practices and doctrines could have played no part in this process. Rather, one is surprised that the Muslims did not borrow more. This demonstrates the exceptionally strong religious self-awareness, the integrity and strength, that characterized the young community of the faithful.

However, it must not be imagined that in demonstrating this *direct* Christian influence one has explained the origin of Sufism. Sufism in effect follows a line which is almost the opposite of the Christian one. The aim of monastic asceticism was to change man from a corporeal and earthly to a spiritual (*pneumatikós*) and heavenly being. When the pious man reaches the state of perfection, he becomes wholly spiritual, like the heavenly light, eternal and divine. The effect of this change may, it is true, be said to signify that he has reached true union of his being with that of God and Christ. But it might also be said, and with equal justification that as a *pneumatikós* he no longer needs either God or Christ; or at least, not the Christ who is proclaimed by the Church. In a manner of speaking, he is himself a Christ. By the process of spiritual self-perfection, man becomes God. Ascetic mysticism represents, in its most characteristic form, the ascending line in religious piety, that is to say, man's striving toward the divine. Sufism moves in the opposite direction. It is not only man's striving for self-perfection that is of importance; above all else it is God who acts, God who intervenes. Herein is love found, not that we have learned to love God, but rather that He has loved us: "The servant would not be able to love God, if God Himself had not begun by first loving him."[72]

Mas'ūdī claims to have read "on the door of a Sabaean house of prayer" in the city of Harran: "He who knows His being, himself becomes divine."[73] There we have the fundamental doctrine of Hellenistic Gnosticism, that the pious man becomes a mortal God.[74] But as we shall see, in Sufism it is not a question of man's metaphysical change into a being of *pneuma* and light, but of a moral change: of becoming, through love, like God in goodness, mercy, truth and faithfulness. It is not that the believing soul by its perfection reaches a state in which, already perfect, it no longer, so to speak, needs God. The more the believer becomes perfected in his love of God, the more he needs Him and Him alone. Catherine of Genoa could confess: "I do not desire Thy gifts, I only desire Thee." And Abū Yazī says: "God gives His servants commandments and prohibitions. When they obey Him, He clothes them in garments of glory, and for the sake of these garments of glory they forget God Himself. From God I want only Himself."[75]

That idyllic state, in which it was not uncommon to find an intimate exchange of spiritual experiences between Christians and Muslims, was characteristic of the first two centuries of Islam. True, even at that stage individual orthodox fanatics could distinguish themselves by bitter intolerance. When Sufyān ath-Thaurī was asked whether it was permissible to greet Jews and Christians, he replied: "Yes, with your foot."[76] But it was only in about AD 800 that an obvious change appeared in the relations between Muslims and Christians. The Abbasid rulers began to apply a Byzantine form of religious policy, including state intervention in religious questions and strict emergency laws to control unacceptable religious minorities. It was a remarkable nemesis of history that the restrictive ordinances the Christian rulers of Byzantium had applied against the Jews were now, under the rule of the Caliphs, turned against the Christians. Previously warm feelings became noticeably cooler, even within the generally open-hearted brotherhood of mystics. The relationship of Islam to Christianity was becoming a thorny problem. It was an inescapable fact that the Christians practiced good works exactly like faithful Muslims, though with even greater zeal and seriousness. Their devotion was acknowledged as exemplary even for Muslims. What, then, ought one to believe? "Even the peoples of the Book advocate a commendable attitude and good deeds. What, then, is the difference between them and us who have the true faith?" asked the disciples of Dhū'n-Nūn. The Master deflects the question with a saying of the noblest tolerance: "He who possesses the true faith is in duty bound to show greater gentleness, forgiveness and tolerance."[77] Others judged the matter more harshly. Muḥāsibī considered that the very works of monastic piety, though admirable in themselves, proved that no man comes to God by works alone. True faith is also necessary.[78] Others hesitated to pronounce such a harsh judgment. Could one really label the monks as infidels, and as such shut off from all communion with God? Dārānī tried to take up a mediating position: "The Christian monks would not be able to endure such renunciation in the deserts and the wildernesses, if they did not experience some spiritual satisfaction in their hearts during their devotional exercises. This is their reward, which God gives them in *this* world. For in the next they will not receive any reward."[79]

Is the Muslim, then, really able to gain spiritual knowledge and edification from Christians, who are known to be infidels? At the beginning of the ninth century AD, writing a work (no longer extant) on the piety of the Christian monks, Burjulānī considered it indeed possible:

> Behold the exhortations of the monks, as well as their works;
> A word of truth, even if it come from the mouths of infidels,
> Is a salutary warning. Let us obey it."[80]

However, such an attitude could not be maintained in the long run. The time was past when the Muslim seeker after God could visit a Christian church to engage in spiritual conversations with the monks. Junayd's disciples asked: "'Are we allowed to go to a church, as a warning to ourselves and to discover the unworthiness of the Christians' unbelief?' He answered: 'If you can go to a church and bring some of the worshippers back with you to the court of God's house, then go, but not otherwise.'"[81]

Thus we encounter a remarkable problem. During a period when direct Christian influence is being reduced to a minimum, the ascetic piety which Islam earlier absorbed from Christianity is being reshaped, as we shall see, in a manner which in a sense can be seen as a drawing closer to the position of Protestant Christianity.

Chapter II

ASCETICISM

"I wish I could eat food that would remain in my stomach like a brick. I have been told that a brick can stay submerged in water for three hundred years without dissolving."[1] This is what Ḥasan al-Baṣrī, the most renowned of pious ascetics during the first century of Islam, is reputed to have said. This, to us, would seem a most peculiar wish. The idea that fasting, deprivation of sleep and other kinds of self-mortification could make us better and more pious, elevating us to a life of greater worth, is totally foreign to us. In that respect, at least, we are good Lutherans. Ḥasan's wish, one day to be able to eat a meal which would liberate him, once and for all, from such an unholy and unspiritual activity as eating, is simply inconceivable to us. We find it very difficult to understand and appreciate a form of religion as sternly ascetical as Christian monastic piety and its offshoots within the earliest community of Islam. In both, the perfect devotee is an emaciated ascetic, dried up like a cracked bag of skin, bent like an archway, so thin that the sun shines through his ribs, red-eyed and with deep furrows in his cheeks from the constant flow of his tears. We may perhaps have a reluctant admiration for the merciless and uncompromising strictness of ascetic spirituality, but can we understand it? What is the root cause of individuals having been able to abuse their own bodies in this way, and violate every healthy and natural urge?

The conscious and rational motives for choosing the ascetic way of life may be of different kinds. In the Gospels the *religious motivation* is dominant. The desire for this world, the love of possessions, earthly joy and bodily pleasure have to be strictly disciplined, if not entirely suppressed, so that they do not intrude between us and God. The motivation of Neo-Platonism and Christian monastic piety is that of *metaphysical dualism*: the body, prison of the soul and original source and home of evil desires, must be subjugated and weakened, in order that the soul may lead a strong and full life. In Stoicism and other moral philosophies we encounter *the motive of asceticism*: a measure of renunciation, perhaps also mortification, may be useful as spiritual exercise. It serves to strengthen and steel the will, and the energy thus dammed up can benefit the spiritual life. But behind all these conscious motives there are, both psychologically and historically speaking, dark and only half-conscious impulses and tendencies toward the life of asceticism. On this point, like so many others in the psychology of religion, it is a matter of remembering the rule that in the beginning was the act, and not the rational motivation for it.

At one stage during my schooldays—it was in the spring term of our fifth year—an epidemic of tattooing went through our class. The tattooing, as we practiced it, was rather a painful process. We drew a monogram or a shape on our arms in ordinary Indian ink, and then, while the outline was still damp, we would make impressions along the outline with a needle, until we were bleeding. It was not so much that we valued the tattoos as such, but one felt especially clever and tough because one had borne and voluntarily submitted to that degree of pain.

It is possible, I believe, that on the occasion there was brought to the surface of our schoolboy souls a brief glimpse of a psychological impulse that has given rise to certain well-known magical rites of self-mortification. When members of Red Indian tribes planned to go to war, they would strengthen themselves by making painful incisions in their arms and legs, by fasting, by depriving themselves of sleep and other harrowing exercises. One observer has remarked that it is hardly possible to imagine a worse method of preparation for an important undertaking than that used by these foolish Indians. However, it is the uncomprehending observer who is foolish, not the Indians. The savages were idealists in their way, for they knew that those spiritual qualities—courage, faith in oneself and fighting spirit—were of greater importance than brute strength. They had suffered and endured something out of the ordinary, something that aroused feelings of competence, ability and power. This subjective feeling was transformed in their minds into objective reality: one really *had* gained a mysterious power, magical knowledge, *mana*.

In India, even at the dawn of time, the holy man would reinforce his supernatural powers by strict ascetic practices: by fasting, mortification and renunciations of various kinds. When one submitted to deprivation and suffering with a ruthless, unnatural severity that would literally terrify normal people with their comfortable habits, one really *felt* oneself to be bursting with supernatural power. The gods themselves feared the ascetic, when by superhuman penances he accumulated *tapas*, "heat," magical power and efficacy. If, in addition, one considers that certain of these exercises, especially fasting and sleep deprivation, resulted in remarkable experiences, such as eidetic vision, hallucinations and trance-like states, in which the soul moves and acts independently and experiences extraordinary things apart from the body, then one many conclude that the basic features of Platonism were already present in the Stone Age: the belief that through mistreatment, discipline and mortification of the body the soul's supernatural power can in certain cases be reinforced.

Thus "ascesis" had arisen at an early stage as a form of action and a method, capable of being used in different contexts for different purposes, magical or religious, with different rational motives, in situations where a human being had to extend the psychological and spiritual limits of his or her natural resources. And in every form of asceticism, including the religious, there is at work, at least as a subsidiary element, the subconscious desire to impress, to gain power in the eyes of those in one's immediate circle, through a pattern of behavior which is unusual, remarkable and arduous. This is not to disparage ascetic piety. However, human action may be determined by societal values and considerations, even when the individual concerned lives as a hermit in a desert cave.

Similar psychological factors are probably at work, at the deepest level, in another type of motivation for the ascetic way of life, a type which, *faute de mieux*, I should like to call the *disciplinary motive*. Life must not be lived at random. Rules and precepts are necessary. It is true that the great moral commandments are there to be kept, but our acts of obedience are neither particularly remarkable nor even encouraging. A man or woman must satisfy that very natural desire to have achieved something, and to be able to feel that he or she has fulfilled a quota of moral obligations. That is why the individual needs a disciplinary practice, a certain self-imposed limitation upon freedom, a certain degree of compulsory renunciation, preferably not too difficult and yet enough to be able to feel that duty has indeed been fulfilled.

This motive is a familiar one, even in non-religious morals. We all know how seriously and scrupulously some people observe the regime of self-imposed diet or hygiene, and the fanatical loyalty shown, for instance, by a vegetarian to his or her principles. It is true that the vegetarian's rational motivation is the conviction that a meat diet is injurious to health. But one may be convinced of the fact that certain habits are medically harmful and yet be totally unable to change them. It would seem that more powerful motives than rational ones are at work here.

The ethics of Islam consists largely of the observance of religious discipline. The entire life of the individual believer is circumscribed by instructions and proscriptions. In addition to the commandments of the Qur'an there are the innumerable directives contained in the Sunna of the Prophet, which regulate the behaviour of the believer in great detail, and at all times. The pious Muslim does not see this as a burden, or as an intolerable limitation upon his freedom. On the contrary, he is proud to know and be able to observe that which the Prophet has commanded, just as many of us are proud of knowing the demands of good manners and anxious to follow strictly the unwritten rules of etiquette.

For the pious Muslim, however, it is not enough merely to obey literally all the prohibitions of the Qur'an and the Sunna. What is permitted and not permitted requires the exercise of discretion, and there are great possibilities for the individual to create a disciplinary observance that accords with his own intentions and to demonstrate a degree of sensitivity of conscience and scrupulousness higher than that of others. More is prohibited than pork and blood. As in early Christianity, there is an injunction against everything that has been bought with money acquired unjustly; there is an injunction against possessing anything to which another person has a more justifiable claim; and against anything which is in any way tainted by sin, wrong and impurity. In such instances one has to find one's own way through a process of free testing of conscience, applied to each individual case. The first generation of ascetics were those from whom the Sufis inherited this view, and the Sufis reinforced such demands, albeit to varying degrees, and made them matters of individual observance. One of the earliest apostles of Sufism, the legendary Ibrāhīm ibn Adham, said: "The one who has any religious merit possesses it, in our opinion, not through pilgrimages nor through participation in the Holy War, but by choosing that which he puts into his stomach from among those things that are permitted."[2] The observance of the rules concerning things forbidden and permitted is more important than all ritual instructions and all spiritual exercises. "As long as you eat only permitted food, it will not matter if you do not deprive yourself of sleep during the night and do not fast during the day."[3]

It is extremely important, even for the adept on the *via mystica*, not to be carelessly negligent concerning what is permitted or forbidden. "He who does not consider it necessary to undertake a careful examination in order to obtain a couple of loaves of bread of permitted foot, it will not go well with him on his road to God," says Dhū'n-Nūn.[4] For the learned traditionalist the question of what is forbidden or permitted is an academic one. He is mainly interested in finding, in every situation, a precedent in the Sunna. For the Sufi the chief concern is his own examination of conscience. To neglect that, testifies to a dereliction of religious duty and to a laxity of the very worst kind: "The pious ones, the ascetics and the reciters of the Qur'an in our day are becoming careless of sin, so that they have sunk into the desires of the flesh and the stomach and are incapable of seeing their own faults. They have begun to eat that which is forbidden and cease to seek permitted food."[5] A zealot such as Yūsuf ibn Asbāṭ was even able to declare that "nine-tenths of piety consists of the search for permitted food."[6] Although not all went to such lengths, several of the classical Sufis distinguished themselves by their strictness in these matters: Bishr, ad-Dārānī, Sahl ibn 'Abdallāh, but above all Sarī as-Saqaṭī, who won praise of Ibn Ḥanbal himself for his scrupulous piety where food was concerned.[7]

The mystic, however, often proves to be more liberal where such minutiae are concerned. The intentions of the heart, the mental attitude, mean more to him than tithes of mint and dill and cummin. It is these other aspects of mystical piety—among them a weakness for the unusual, the *recherché* and the complicated, even in the case of ethical ideals; scrupulousness; hypersensitivity of conscience and the penchant towards subtle self-examination—that lead to this apparent inconsistency. Such a view of the dietary question is easily adopted by the oriental mind even in our day. When Gandhi travelled to England, he took his own goat with him and lived on her milk, as well as on tomatoes and oranges. To millions of his countrymen, his sanctity and spiritual authority were certainly connected in some way with the fact that he consumed only "permitted" food. The idea of a Mahatma in a restaurant, eating the same food as ordinary, secular mortals is inconceivable to the Indian mind.

There were traditional rules in Islam laying down what is permissible. Legally pure and good is that which is gained through fair dealing, the honest work of one's hands, and lawful gift. And a lawful gift is: booty won by the faithful in a holy war, a gift given with a generous heart, and alms given for the sake of God.[8] According to Sarī, the food of the devoted Muslim, as well as the money for which it is bought, should be free of the following faults: the sins of commerce; the humiliation of begging; the tricks and deceptions of trade; the use of the tools of disobedience; the dependence upon godless princes.[9] The ideal is to consume only those things "for which one does not need to give account to God, and for which one is not indebted to any man." But many devout Muslims would have to give up hope of being able to find such food. Everything which has passed through human hands is tainted with sin and impurity. If possible one should therefore eat only that which grows in ground that has no owner, and drink the rain that falls from heaven. That which is given by Nature comes straight from the hand of God.

A wandering ascetic once met a holy man and invited him to share his food, but he refused to taste it: "We holy men eat only that which is permitted, and by this means our hearts are strengthened to renounce and perpetually remain in that same state in which we can see that kingdom which is hidden and the world that is to come."

The other man said: "I fast constantly and recite the Qur'an from beginning to end, thirty times a month."

The holy man replied: "I treasure that which you now see me drinking more highly than a thousand readings of the Qur'an and three hundred prostrations." What he was drinking was the milk of a wild antelope.

But the visitor continued: "You saints live on permitted food, and yet you do not care about feeding your brethren among the faithful."

The ascetic replied: "Our way of life does not suit everyone. If everyone were to eat only that which is permitted, then society would founder, the market places would be empty and the kingdoms devastated. We are only a small number of chosen people, who have received God's command to live like this."[10] No food could be more untainted by the world than the milk of the wild antelope. How exquisitely holy and spiritual that individual must become who lives solely on such drink!

The eating of permitted food even creates, *ex opere operato*, a wonderful predisposition toward piety and devotion. It makes a person stronger in prayer.[11] Sahl explains that "he who eats that which is forbidden, the members of his body become disobedient, whether he wants it or not. But he who eats only permitted food, his members become obedient and disposed to do good."[12] However, no food is permitted which is not consumed with the intention of strengthening the pious Muslim for the service of God, "not even if you open your mouth toward heaven and drink the falling rain."[13]

A friend came to Sarī as-Saqaṭī and found him weeping, because his clay pot had broken. Desiring to comfort him, the friend said: "I shall buy you another to replace it." But Sarī was inconsolable: "You are going to buy me another one! Just think of it, that in the case of that pot I knew where the money came from, that I paid for it. I knew where the clay came from, and what the potter had to eat while he worked, until he had finished the pot."[14] Thus that pot was completely pure and safe, and consequently irreplaceable. The believer must be equally careful about everything that he uses for food, drink and household utensils. One must ask and ask again, until one is completely convinced. Wuhayb ibn Ward did not eat any food, if he had not received testimony from two witnesses that it was pure and safe to eat.

Abū Sulaymān ad-Dārānī tells us that if at any time he had eaten questionable food, that is, food that had not been proved clean, he felt "a fire in his heart from one Friday to the next."[15] Others would feel a similar inner warning. Everything that arouses disquiet in our souls and minds is sin, but that action or that thing which brings to our hearts a feeling of security and peace, is good. Yūsuf ibn Asbāṭ and others who kept to a stricter observance abstained from anything which would cause such disquiet of mind. It is not crass selfishness, but only wise caution which is expressed in the following rule: That which one receives and obtains which is pure and good and raised above every doubt, that the pious Muslim may use for food and clothing for his family or for the upkeep of his household in other ways: firewood, rent, furnishing fabrics and other furniture.[16] It is in fact only the chosen one who is subject to the full severity of the commandment concerning permissible foods. That which his elevated and sensitive spirituality cannot endure, may be completely safe to the constitution of an ordinary secular human being.

It did not take a great deal to arouse the apprehensions of the devoted Muslim. 'Abdallāh ibn Mubārak had a female dove, whose young were raised by his family and then killed for the household dinner table. But one day a strange male dove arrived and copulated with her several times. From that on, 'Abdallāh refused to eat any bird from her brood,[17] either because he was offended by the wantonness of the dove or because he suspected the strange dove of bringing with it some taint of sin from a house of unbelievers. Another pious man had a ewe which on one occasion happened to eat a few pieces of straw, fodder which belonged to the Emir of Mecca. He never again drank that ewe's milk.[18] It is especially sinful and dangerous to receive anything from godless rulers and princes. Bishr, who was reputed to be a saint, considered himself too pious to work for a living. His sister then had to support him by spinning wool. One evening, as she sat spinning wool on the roof, the servants of the governor rode past, carrying burning torches. Afterwards she turned to Ibn Ḥanbal and asked him if the skein of wool which she had been spinning on the spindle that night could be used to support the holy man, since a length of the thread had been spun in the light from an unbeliever's torches.[19] Sulaymān at-Taymī would not eat bread baked from flour which had been ground in a water-mill. All the faithful had an equal share in the water, it is true, but the mill-owners had selfishly laid their hands on the income from the mill.[20] Another pious Muslim was especially afraid of eating anything which had been cursed. He paid his cook two or three *dirham* a month, so that the cook should not curse the food, if he happened to burn himself on the stove or the cooking-pot.[21]

If one makes such severe demands, it must be difficult to find any pure and untainted food at all. One day, during a military expedition, Sarī came to a green meadow where he found some wild lettuce and where rainwater had collected in hollowed-out stones. He thought: "If ever in my life I were able to eat permitted food, it would be now." But when he dismounted from his horse to start eating, he heard a voice saying: "Sarī! But where did the money come from, which you used for your journey to this place?"[22] Particularly in these latter days—after the year AH 200–810 AD, when dishonesty, treachery, and evil have gained the upper hand among people—it had become almost impossible to find any untainted food.[23] One should therefore, says Sahl, be content with only that amount of food and drink which is absolutely necessary to sustain life.[24] One should nevertheless honestly carry out the testing of one's conscience and for the rest trust in God's power always to protect His friends from evil and impurity. "For if all the earth were one single pool of blood, even so the nourishment which God gives to the faithful from her would be pure and permitted."[25]

There were of course many among the faithful who would resolutely disregard these scruples. Yaḥyā ibn Maʿīn aroused extreme displeasure when he declared: "I do not ask anyone for anything, but if Satan himself were to give me something, I would eat it."[26] However, the earliest Sufis generally regarded the scrupulous testing of food as an expression of the *wara'* of the faithful, that is, that negative piety which leads to a fear of performing any wrong or evil act.[27]

One of the Old Pietist preachers in the country area where I grew up was walking to church one Sunday morning, his mind filled with pious thoughts. Suddenly he discovered a piece of straw on his fine, black Sunday overcoat. And that piece of straw caused him acute problems of conscience. If he were to brush it off, he argued, that would be a sign of pride and worldliness: to be thinking of grooming oneself for other people, while going to the house of God. If he left it there, that might be spiritual pride: wanting to be better than others. This was one difference between the Old Pietist and the New Evangelicals. The former required a strict self-examination in any situation of possible sin, according the pattern: Do I perhaps enjoy the praise of worldly men? However, I grieve over the fact that I enjoy it. But maybe I enjoy the very grief . . . and so on. Several of the earliest Sufis knew this excessive tenderness of conscience. One day Dāwūd aṭ-Ṭāʾī rested in the burning sun, because he was not certain whether moving into the shade might not possibly be a sin.[28] Sarī said: "If someone comes to visit me and I stroke my beard with my hand to smooth it, I fear that this act may be a sin which condemns me to hell."[29] Concerning another of "the anxiously pious ones," *al-wāriʿūn*, there is a story that on one occasion he dropped a gold coin. When he bend down to pick it up, he found two gold coins on the ground. He thought: "I do not know which of them is mine. I might unwittingly acquire someone else's property." And so he left both coins lying there.[30] The importance of the problem of what is permitted and what is not in Sufi asceticism must be regarded as a reflect of this tendency toward scrupulous self-examination.

Among the subconscious impulses toward self-mortification and renunciation certain modern psychologists have emphasized one in particular, namely, the sexual motive. According to J.H. Leuba, for example, the ecstasy of mystical love is always, or at least commonly, based on suppressed sexuality. Its negative opposite, the excruciating pain which the mystics speak of so frequently and which alternates with ecstatic bliss, is based on strong sexual arousal, which is not permitted natural release. In such a situation this irrestible inner pressure seeks release in excessive self-mortification. Egyptian monks would expose their naked bodies to the merciless desert sun, for the same reason that soeur Jeanne des Anges could spend the night naked in the snow: in order to chill the ardour of concupiscence. No doubt Muslim mysticism may be of more general interest in this light, for unlike early Christianity Islam did not demand any suppression of sensuality, and the believer therefore did not need to suffer the consequences of sexual repression, at least not for religious reasons.

Muhammad himself, as we know, did not count sexual abstinence among the religious virtues. The Prophet had been given permission, as a special prerogative, to marry nine wives. An ordinary man had to content himself with four, though he had the right instead to divorce his wife when he pleased, and marry another. This is how Ḥasan, Muhammad's grandson, was able to marry 250 times. His fickleness was so notorious that his father, the Caliph ʿAlī, who had himself been married ten times, and in addition had fourteen concubines, found it embarrassing. Many of the pious Fathers of Islam permitted themselves a liberty similar to that exercised by the patriarchs of Mormonism, Joseph Smith and

Brigham Young. The Islamic attitude to marriage may be summed up as follows: marriage is an absolute duty for everyone who needs it in order to live chastely, and should be entered into by anyone who can afford it. This being so, it is rather surprising that there have been any celibates at all in Islam. It is a well-known fact that in Christian monastic piety the first rule of asceticism was to observe strict sexual abstinence. Evil lust, concupiscence, *is* sexual desire. The influence of monastic religion was in fact so powerful, that individual ascetics within Islam not only accepted the doctrine of celibacy in principle but also practiced it. It is true that they were few in number and seem to have been considered eccentrics, odd exceptions to the rule, and were not very highly regarded. Occasionally such pious eccentrics were brought before the Caliph on charges of heresy, on the grounds of their unwillingness to submit to the Prophet's Sunna. More commonly, pious ascetics and mystics openly praised the spiritual and worldly advantages of the unmarried state, and emphasized marriage and women as a great hindrance to a life of true religious devotion, while not living according to those principles.

The guile and deceit of women is a well-loved theme in this extremely patriarchal society—a society in which everything, including religion, is seen from an exclusively male point of view and in which misogyny flourishes as the natural obverse of a very great weakness for the female sex. Devotional literature, too, is full of lamentations over women and their destructive influence. Female advice leads to evil consequences: "In this age no man obeys his wife in all that she wishes; if he does, God consigns him headlong into hell."[33] A woman's guile, when she desires to bring a man under her control, is profound and inscrutable. Arabian mothers gave their marriageable daughters the following advice: "My daughter, test your friend, before you give yourself to him. First take the point of his lance. If he keeps silent, cut some meat with it on his shield. If he still remains silent, take his sword and crush some bones with it. If he does not say a word even at this point, put a saddle on his back and use him as your beast of burden, for he is an ass."[32] Woman is often man's punishment and misfortune. One of those who suffered most, was Yūnus ibn Mattā, the prophet Jonah. One day he was visited by some fellow believers whom he invited, in accordance with the custom of brotherhood, to share his meal. He was forced to prepare the food himself, but that was not all; while he ran back and forth performing his domestic duties, his wife kept nagging him and heaping insults upon him. When his brethren expressed their surprise that he was prepared to accept this treatment, Jonah replied: "Many years ago I besought God that He would allow me in this world to suffer the punishment He had prepared for me in the world to come. God answered: 'Your punishment is a woman whose name is So-and-So. Take her in marriage.' This have I done, and now I am suffering my punishment."[33]

Most women have little religion and little honesty. "In women there is united the unbelief both of past and present generations."[34] Generally they are ruled by ignorance and evil desires. A pious woman is as rare as a white raven. Therefore one should keep women on a taut rein. Even Shāfiʿī, the famous lawyer, is reputed to have given vent to the following unchivalrous opinion: "Three kinds of being are made in such a way that if you honour them, they will despise you, but if you despise them, they will honour you. They are: foreigners, slaves and women."[35] Above all else, a pious believer must be on his guard against the seductresses. Saʿīd ibn al-Musayyib confessed, even at the age of eighty-four: "There is nothing I fear as much as women."[36]

Having a family to look after hinders and distracts the pious believer in his devotion. Therefore it is said: "When God looks favourably upon a servant, he allows his wife to die and leaves him on his own to devote himself to the worship of God."[37] Muwarraq al-ʻIjlī went even further in holy selfishness: "Of all those things that might befall me, nothing would please me more than the death of my wife."[38] Mālik ibn Dīnār, to whom we have referred earlier as being especially well acquainted with Christian literature, expresses a similar thought but chooses his words more carefully: "O God, do not vouchsafe me property, nor children, and if you have given me anything which does not please you, then take it away from me."[39] Mālik totally opposed the idea of marriage in the case of the elect believer. When asked whether he intended to marry, he replied: "Were I able to divorce my own self, I would."[40] However, he had been married once, and then, in blind infatuation, he had bought one *dirham's* (fifty cents') worth of scent for his wife, an act of extravagance which he regretted for twenty years.[41] Perhaps he was remembering painful personal experiences when he warned the readers of the Qur'an: "A man divorces his wife and marries a beautiful woman, a princess from Byzantium or a girl whom her father has fattened up, so that she has grown soft and white as foam. She captivates his heart completely, so that he asks her: 'What do you wish for?' and she answers: 'Such-and-such a thing.' By Allah, that man's religion is sick."[42] He held it permissible for the believer engaged in the quest for perfection (though not for the ordinary Muslim) to leave his family to look after themselves as best they could: "A man has not been numbered among the righteous until he has left his wife like a widow and his children like orphans and sought refuge among the dogs."[43] Rabīʻ boasted that he knew the sparrows in the mosque more intimately than he knew his wife.[44]

In the world of Islam children are welcomed as a gift of God. Ibrāhīm ibn Adham himself says that Moses asked God one day: "Among all acts of piety, which one pleases You most?" The Lord answered: "Kindness to children. For children rejoice My heart."[45] Above all, it is a man's pride and joy to have a son. But even this feeling must be suppressed by the true ascetic. As in the Egyptian monastic fathers or the saints of Roman Catholic monasteries, it is indeed proof of heroic devotion to show lack of feeling towards one's children. It happened that a Sufi's little son had lost his way and disappeared. For three days he had heard nothing from the boy. Then someone asked the father: "Will you not pray to God, that He give you back your son?" But he answered: "To blame God for something that He has done is worse, to my mind, than to lament the loss of my son."[46] When Rābi'a, a famous woman mystic, saw one of her brethren hug and kiss his little son, she said: "I really did not believe that there was room in your heart for the love of anyone but God."[47] One of Sufyān ath-Thaurī's sons came to his father's reading one day, having been sent by his mother, and sat down in front of him. But Sufyān said: "O, that I were called to your funeral." Shortly thereafter he did in fact have to bury him.[48] Sufyān warned his disciples against the temptations of love: "It will never go well with the one who accustoms himself to the embraces of women."[49] In his opinion marriage meant constant worry and worldly troubles. The unmarried man keeps the most precious of all possessions, his peace of soul:

> How blessed is the single man's lot! He owns a safe haven. However angrily the tempest is raging, its noise and disturbance will not reach him there.[50]

One second-century ascetic was even of the opinion that a man, if he could manage without a woman, should cut his throat rather than marry a woman.[51] If one is not able to realize the ideal of celibacy, one should at least be content with *one* wife and remember that the faithful believer will be granted compensation in paradise: "God is merciful to the man who contents himself with one wife, even if she is middle-aged and looks unpleasant, if he sincerely believes (the promise of) women in paradise."[52]

These Sufis contrive to evade one issue fairly comfortably, that is the somewhat embarrassing fact that the Prophet had indeed stressed marriage as a duty. This command was applicable to the Prophet's own day, when women were better and more religious than latterly, and when they made fewer demands on life. In these evil and corrupt days (the Sufis explained), celibacy is not only permitted, but the single man has also a definite advantage over the married man, since the Prophet is reputed to have said: "After two hundred years celibacy shall be permitted in my community." For in the latter days women will become even more troublesome and wicked than they are already by nature. The woman will despise her husband for his poverty and force him to take up dishonest and dangerous occupations and sources of income, in order to satisfy her desire for luxuries. There is a clear echo of a text from the Gospels in the following words: "The time will come, when a man's wife and his son and his parents will cause his spiritual ruin. In that day it will be better for a man to raise a cat or a dog than to bring up a son." In conclusion it is conceded that marriage is better for anyone who is otherwise unable to govern his desires. "But for the believer who does not suffer such overpowering temptations it is best to remain single. For in his solitude he is able to occupy himself with his own soul, his own desires and his own enemy."[53] Thus the permission to marry is a concession to uncontrollable human nature. On that point, Islam approaches the Pauline view fairly closely: "He who marries his betrothed does well, and he who refrains from marriage does better" (A. Cor. 7:38).

There existed among the earlier ascetics in Islam a considerable body of opinion in favor of celibacy, or at any rate an ethical and religious discrimination against marriage and family life. However, these were in fact isolated voices, which drew attention to themselves all the more since they ran counter to general opinion. For the majority, even among those who practiced a stricter piety, kept firmly to the view that it was the duty of all the faithful to marry. If a man becomes a widower, he should remarry without delay, "for God has cursed those men and women who live in celibacy." Ibn Mas'ūd declared: "Even if I knew that I had only ten days left of my life, I would still remarry, to avoid going to meet God as a single man."[54] There is a resemblance here to the practice of the Old Lutherans in Sweden, as described by Troels Lund.[55] In their case the rules stipulated that the year of mourning must pass before a new marriage was contracted; however, this period of delay should be used to arrange and prepare the matter in advance. It sometimes happened that the widower would start a new courtship immediately after his wife's funeral.

Muslims generally did not hesitate to take full advantage of the liberty allowed by Islamic law. God has permitted the believer to have four wives, and has done so with a view to the four temperaments, which are part of human character. For each temperament a man ought to have a wife suited to its particular tendencies and inclinations. The fact that the woman's character also includes four temperaments, which perhaps also require their erotic counterpart, was something which the law unfortunately did not consider. Attempts were also made to prove by means of other comparisons, that were ingenious rather than tasteful, that the particular number of four had been especially wisely chosen. If a man owns four shirts, that is *not* wasteful, but it would be, if he had more than four. Also, God has created four species of animals for man to ride on: the horse, the camel, the mule and the donkey. Therefore the man should also be granted four wives.[56]

One ought to marry and have children in order to extend the community of Muhammad. If a man has a son, it may be assumed that he will grow up and become one of the faithful. Or else he will die, and in that case he will save his parents on the Day of Judgment, for God is merciful to little children and opens the gates of Paradise to them without trial or judgment. But the children stay by the gates crying, refusing to enter without their parents. Then God will, for the sake of the children, overlook that which is still lacking in the parents' balance of good works, and will allow them to accompany their little ones into Paradise.[57]

Work in support of one's family does not necessarily signify an intrusion in a man's spiritual life. On the contrary, it is such a great work and so pleasing in the sight of God, that a married man even has the right to abstain from the communal prayer for the sake of gainful employment. Not only is the one who deserts his family a man without honor; he also lacks devotion. He is like a runaway slave. God will accept neither his prayer nor his fasting until he returns to his duty.[58] ᶜAbdallāh ibn Mubārak, one of the closest precursors of the Sufis, was a pious man of the old school. Although he was prosperous and independent, he fulfilled his personal duty to participate in the war against the enemies of the faith. One day, encamped with some of his fellow-believers, he asked them: "Do you know of any work that is more pleasing before God than the one we are now engaged in?" They answered that they did not. He continued: "But I know one: when a pious man, who has many children, gets up and sees his little ones sleeping without a blanket and then spreads his own cloak over them to protect them against the cold. What he does is better than what we are doing."[59]

How, then, did the great classical Sufis regard marriage, positively or negatively? It may be pointed out, to begin with, that there are only two famous Sufis, Ibrāhīm ibn Adham and Abū Yazīd al-Bisṭāmī, who are definitely known to have been celibates. Also Dāwūd aṭ-Ṭā'ī "lived celibate for sixty-four years." When asked how he could endure a life without women, he said: "I overcame my desire for them when I reached manhood. After that, the desire vanished."[60] Dāwūd however belonged to the precursors of Sufism. Ibrāhīm ibn Adham did not reject marriage in principle, but made a personal choice not to marry. He had no desire for women and thought that if he were to marry, he would have to disappoint his wife's expectations, when she asked him for earthly love. He did not on the other hand value celibacy higher, spiritually, than marriage. A man once said to him: "How fortunate you are to be unmarried and able to devote yourself entirely to the worship of God." But Ibrāhīm answered: "Your worry and care where your family is concerned is better than all my pious devotion."[61] Abū Yazīd said that he had intended to ask God to liberate him from the need for food and women. But he thought it presumptuous to pray for something which the Prophet himself had not dared to ask. "Thus I did not pray for it. Yet God liberated me from the need for women, so that it is the same to me whether I walk past a woman or a wall."[62]

Bishr had been married,[63] but after the dissolution of that marriage he lived alone. He was a solitary man and he always trod the narrow path. "He is as if poised on the point of a lance," said Aḥmad ibn Ḥanbal.[64] When he was asked if he would not follow the Sunna on the Prophet and remarry, he said: "My duty to obey God's commandments makes it impossible for me to follow the Prophet's Sunna." Bishr was another Sufi who did not dare to take a stand for celibacy as a principle, but he was hardly averse to describing it as the higher choice: "He who does not need women should worship God and not accustom himself to their embraces. But if a man has four wives, whom he really needs, than that is not excessive."[65] Al-Ghazālī's precursor Abū Ṭālib al-Makkī shared Bishr's opinion. In a statement which can hardly be said to accord with orthodox Sunna, he explains: "God has neither prescribed marriage nor celibacy, nor has he made it a duty to have four wives. He has commanded us to keep our hearts honest and good, and see to it that we are able to keep the faith and seek our souls' peace. For him who is best able to maintain his spiritual health and inner peace through having four wives, it is permitted to live in a fourfold marriage. For the one who finds one wife enough, monogamy is best. And he whose spiritual life and inner peace is best served by celibacy, will feel most secure living as a celibate."[66]

On the question of marriage, Abū Sulaymān took up a position similar to that of those earlier ascetics who would warn against the religious dangers and worldly difficulties of the married state, but did not themselves live as celibates. He lamented that his family hindered and distracted him in his devotion,[67] judging the joy of having children with a monk's harshness: "He who wants a son is a fool. Whether he wants to eat or sleep or make love, he will disturb him. If he wants to devote himself to worship, the son occupies his thoughts."[68] He had observed that his disciples, as soon as they married, descended a few steps on the ladder of spiritual rank and perfection. "What the single man is able to experience of the bliss of adoration and of the undisturbed devotion of the heart, the married man will never know."[69] Now, if one must necessarily marry, one should at least practise asceticism to the extent that one marries an old, poor and ugly woman rather than one who is young, beautiful and rich.[70] Abū Sulaymān judged women more bitterly than anyone else: "It is easier to tolerate a life without women than to endure living with them. For enduring them is worse than hell itself."[71] However, he revealed his innermost feelings in a sigh from the heart: "Nothing in the world is greater bliss than women."[72]

Abū Sulaymān's disciples apparently did not take his warning against marriage very seriously. His favorite disciple and spiritual heir, Aḥmad ibn Abī'l-Ḥawārī, had four wives; apart from a more spiritual marriage with the beautiful but morally strict Rābi'a, herself a famous Sufi saint, there were three others.[72] Ḥātim al-Aṣamm, by contrast, had a fairly severe and legalistic view of the way of the mystic. It begins with a fourfold death: white, black, red and green, or in other words, to endure hunger, suffer insults, struggle against the self and wear the mantle sown together from rags. But where love was concerned, he was no ascetic. In his own words: "I have four wives and nine children! O, how the devil desires to lead me into temptation by forcing me to worry about their keep."[74] However, Ḥātim held marriage in high esteem, as is clear from the following maxim taught by him to his disciples: "All hurry is of the devil, except in three cases: when it is a matter of bringing in food for a guest, paying a debt and giving a grown-up daughter in marriage."[75]

Sahl was a strong advocate of severely ascetical practices and had developed into a virtuoso in the art of fasting, by systematically depriving himself of food. But where women were concerned one should not in his opinion practice asceticism, "for the lord of ascetics (the Prophet himself) loved them".[76] The Qur'an subsumes wife, children and property under one heading as entities of equal worth among those worldly things which must not be allowed to bind the servant of God. Sahl drew a sharp distinction: "He who loves money does not love the next world, and he who loves his food does not love God. But love of parents and children does not drive out the love of God from his heart. God himself has planted it in a man's heart as a natural disposition. Neither is love for God excluded by your love for your wife, in so far as it signifies goodness and tenderness toward her. The same applies to the desire for worldly success and happiness in all those things which are absolutely needful for the soul and the body. For the love of God belongs to the realm of faith, but the love of these other things falls within the area of reason."[77]

There is a thus a purely human system of morals, a *iustitia civilis*, which has its given sphere and its own justification, as long as it does not come into conflict with the realm of faith. A positive evaluation of marriage and family life emerges more and more markedly in the second generation of Sufi teachers. The type of heroic devotion which expresses itself in a lack of feeling toward wife and children does not arouse Tirmidhī's admiration. He narrates a touching piece of oral tradition: one day 'Alī and Fāṭima gave the very last of their stock of flour to a poor man and an orphan, leaving their own little children to go hungry for three days. One can imagine the scene: the holy family themselves, Ḥasan and Ḥusayn, crying with hunger! But Tirmidhī coldly explains that that story must be untrue. 'Alī must have known that the father of a family is obliged to look after his own, before he gives anything away.[78]

Thus, although individual Sufis occasionally let slip a word about the difficulties of marriage, it was not meant to be taken too seriously. It rather seems to be, if one may be forgiven such an irreverent expression, a type of pious snobbery. Their practical attitude was quite different. Their critics maintained that the Sufis possessed three outstanding qualities: they enjoyed food, sweet things and women. Junayd came to their defense with arguments familiar from other discussions about the weaknesses of pious believers. They fast, he says, from time to time in a very strict and disciplined manner, and therefore they satisfy their appetites all the more enthusiastically when they allow themselves the opportunity. They take the injunction against drinking wine with the utmost seriousness, and hence are very fond of sweets—a habit which present-day teetotallers have been reputed to share. Finally, with regard to their fondness of the female sex, one ought to remember that they keep their desires strictly under control, where forbidden love is concerned.[79] Junayd himself took a somewhat crass view of marriage, almost in the style of Stiernhielm: "I need a wife like I need food."[80] He recommended celibacy only to the beginner on the *via mystica*, during his years of apprenticeship.[81]

Marriage has moral value also because it is a hard school and greatly educative for a man's character. "Woman requires a large measure of gentle consideration, noble wisdom, goodness, generosity, a friendly manner and kind words." If you marry a good woman, marriage may even be counted as a work of piety and a way of reaching the future life. What a husband in such a case spends on his wife, is put into the balance of his good words, together with the alms that he has given, and he will be rewarded for every piece of food that he puts into her mouth.[82]

It is hard to believe it, when one has seen the contempt with which women were often treated in Islamic culture, but it is nevertheless a fact that piety in a woman is estimated exceptionally highly: one wayward woman is worse than a hundred promiscuous men. Conversely, one pious woman will receive the same reward as hundred pious men.[83] Her temptations are greater, her powers of resistance less. The annals of Sufism speak of many pious women, some of whom were admired as saints, and who exercised extensive influence. Fāṭima of Nīshāpūr spent her life mostly as a pious pilgrim in Jerusalem or Mecca. The best-known mystics of her day, Dhū'n-Nūn and Abū Yazīd, would ask her advice in spiritual matters and were astonished at her profound spiritual insight. Another Fāṭima was the daughter of the governor of Balkh and had married a Sūfī sheikh in order to find her way to God through him. But she also had Abū Yazīd as her spiritual director. She was very free and informal in her behavior toward him and even showed herself in his presence without a veil, with the consequence that her husband became jealous. One day, however, Abū Yazīd happened to notice that she had begun to color her fingertips with henna and asked her why she had done so. Then Fāṭima said: "O Bāyazīd, so long as you did not see my hand and the henna I was at my ease with you, but now that your eye has fallen on me our compansionship is unlawful."[84]

Thus it is clear that during the very centuries when the dour transcendental religion of Islam was opening out into the flower of mysticism, into glowing and ecstatic devotion to God, the influence of Christian monastic religion and its ideal of celibacy was being greatly reduced. Most of these mystics were married, and several of them had more than one wife. This is undoubtedly a fact to remember for those psychologists who believe themselves to have solved the riddle of mystical devotion in terms of repressed and stifled sexual urges.

At the beginning of this chapter I asked why people should submit to an ascetic regime which often brutally violates their natural instincts. The human being is basically fairly reasonable and calculating, at least where his or her own interests are concerned. It is obvious that it is not for nothing that he or she submits to almost superhuman sacrifices and deprivations. He or she expects to gain something in return. One will never be able to understand mysticism if one does not take into account the fact that the method of renouncing this world to find the next is powerfully supported by a definite inner experience. By self-mortification and above all by fasting and deprivation of sleep the pious believer achieves, at any rate psychologically, real contact with another world. Previously unknown powers and abilities are gained by one who is otherwise "of the early earthy," that is, to be able to see the invisible, to experience the ineffable and to feel a happiness which in its highest form can only be called bliss. He or she reaches that state which we call trance, rapture, ecstasy. Psychologists have also studied these phenomena experimentally, after finding that in a number of cases of hysterically induced illness, states appeared which at least resemble the ones we have spoken of here. By this means psychologists may perhaps imagine that religious ecstasy has been "explained". In their opinion it is a relatively simple mechanism that is at work here: that is, a gradual narrowing-down of consciousness through voluntary or forced concentration, mono-ideism and finally trance.

Of course, nothing has in fact been "explained" by such comparisons. States of consciousness are not mechanisms of such a nature that if you know how one of them functions, you therefore know everything about all the rest. They always contain one factor which is incomparable and at the deepest level inaccessible: the personality, that particular composition of the unified stream of consciousness, of which the various states are phases, or transitory manifestations. From similar observable reactions one deduces a similar inner definition, but this is a conclusion which can, at best, be probable in some cases, but certainly not in every case. The ecstasy of St. Theresa, the trance which the medicine man (shaman) achieves by beating a drum and drinking tobacco juice, and the quiet slumber of the spiritist medium *is not* one and the same experience. And the comparison will certainly not tell us anything about the immeasurable feelings of joy and spiritual worth which Theresa experienced. Therefore I regard it as highly unlikely that those sensations of bliss experienced by Janets' hysterical patients as some kind of by-product of their disease, will tell us anything about that state of bliss and spiritual exaltation which healthy human beings, who have devoted long years of their lives to exercises in the hard school of ascesis, may have gained as their reward. To judge from the incomparably higher price that they have paid, one is inclined to assume that the subjective value of their experiences must have been immeasurably greater. I therefore consider that honesty and wisdom require us to concede that we do not know, nor are we properly able to know, the nature of that experience of bliss acquired by the mystic for the bitter price of ascesis. If we knew it, then perhaps some of us would become adepts in the strenuous art of fasting and self-denial.

It is however certain that the desire to reach such a state has been one of the deepest and most effective motives—not, it is true, a clearly conscious motive, but nonetheless a real one—for the practice of ascesis. This must have been especially true of fasting and deprivation of sleep, two methods which experience has proved to be particularly effective means of opening the transcendental world of the soul.

If celibacy is the first commandment for those wishing to follow the monastic way, then fasting is the second commandment. To pamper and fatten the flesh is the death of the spirit. A spiritual human being (*pneumatikós*) ought ideally to renounce all earthly food. Stories are told concerning holy fathers in the desert who had reached the point of living exclusively on the eucharistic bread. Abba Isodoros wept, because he had not reached that stage, but "although a rational being (he) still consumed the food of the irrational beings." In this, as in other respects, Muslim ascetics would follow the practices of the Christian hermits without closer reflection as to their spiritual motives. To eat only bread and salt was the strict discipline of fasting followed by the monks. On this diet many Muslim ascetics whom we know by name, lived for years. "Eat bread with salt, it reduces the kidney fat and gives increase of faith." However, there was an even stricter school, of those who considered even such a minimal diet an indulgence: "He who not only asks for bread, but also wants salt with his bread, cannot follow the way of the people of God successfully."[85]

Many Sufis were also in this respect faithful followers of their precursors among the ascetics of the early period. Fasting retained its place among the works of piety, but the motivation for it was subject to marked changes and showed strikingly personal variations. Abū Sulaymān ad-Dārānī valued fasting highly as a spiritual exercise: "The best that I have ever been, was when my stomach stuck to my back through starvation."[86] To go without the evening meal and then to sleep is better than to satisfy one's hunger and then spend the whole night in prayer.[87] Fasting had become to him an inclination and a regular habit. He thought that if the believer were allowed to follow his inclination freely, his body would succumb from the lack of food. "Nothing in the world is dearer to me than being able to content myself with that which is absolutely needful to sustain life."[88] Because he himself fasted voluntarily and ate with reluctance, he warned against exaggerated ideas about the spiritual value of fasting. To suppress one single desire of the self is better than fasting for a whole year.[89]

To be able to go without food is a special and miraculous gift, given by God to those pious believers who have reached the stage of perfection.[90] It comes when faith has grown strong enough. "The farther one has come in the certainty of faith (*yaqīn*), the less food one needs." God punishes the unbeliever by giving him a voracious appetite: "He must fill seven bellies, while the believer only needs to fill one."[91]

Individual Sufis, like the Indian fakirs, developed fasting into a veritable art. None of the famous Sufi teachers attached so great importance to fasting as did Sahl ibn 'Abdallāh. To have abstained from all unnecessary eating would, in his opinion, count for more on the Day of Judgment than all other pious works and devotional exercises. Everything that exceeds one third of a normal daily ration he counts as unnecessary. He who eats more, eats up his good works.[92] Personally he was content with far less. Through a sophisticated method of diminishing his daily rations gradually, he arrived at a point where he was finally able to fast for twenty-five days, and sometimes even longer. He speaks about this himself: "I divide my intelligence and my knowledge and my strength into seven parts. Then I abstain from eating, until six-sevenths have disappeared and only one-seventh remains. Because I am afraid that this part also will disappear, and my life with it, I eat enough to stay alive and thus I regain the lost six-sevenths."[93] As we see, he did not practice fasting constantly, as the earlier ascetics had done, but temporarily, as a particular spiritual exercise, much as Gandhi fasted in order to achieve a definite goal. The wise Mahatma would seem to have discovered at an early stage that the hunger strike could be an excellent means of applying pressure to the British authorities; however, his intention at the outset was probably to concentrate and to strengthen his powers of soul and mind to their highest degree of spiritual efficiency. From what we know of Junayd's disciples it is clear that such periodic fasting was common among the Sufis. That is probably why one often finds contradictory information concerning the fasts of individual Sufi saints. Ibrāhīm ibn Adham spent a period of time at the mosque in Basra. During his stay he would only eat every third evening. On the nights when he broke his fast, he wandered about like a Buddhist monk, begging for food at the doors.[94] At other times, he put so much food on his table that he was accused of extravagance.[95]

There is no lack of examples to show that Muslim ascetics found everything to do with the act of eating unclean and unholy. The great traditionalist al-Bukhārī limited his food intake to one date or one nut a day, out of fear that he might happen to eat something forbidden, but also because he was ashamed of going to the latrine in the sight of God.[96] Dāwūd aṭ-Ṭā'ī ate only breadcrumbs soaked in water, in order to get through the process of eating as quickly as possible. "In the time that it takes to chew the bread, I could have read 50 verses."[97] For the same reason another ascetic never ate baked bread, but only flour.[98] But it was not the eating in itself that was sinful to the Sufis. It is satiety which makes the soul slow and prone to sin. Dhū'n-Nūn confessed: "I have never satisfied my hunger without sinning or thinking of sin."[99] Above all, satiety arouses carnal desire. Abū Sulaymān one day walked through a field of wheat and watched a pair of birds greedily picking up the fallen grains. When they were full, the male felt desire for the female. "Behold," said the holy man to his disciple, "how their stomachs tempt them, when they have satisfied their hunger."[100] Otherwise, the aim of the Sufi discipline of fasting is above all to strengthen the spiritual powers of the soul and open it to inspiration from above. "Hunger is a cloud," says Abū Yazīd, "when the heart is hungry, it rains wisdom."[101] "Hunger is light, but satiety is fire."[102] Fasting is the key to the unseen world. When Sahl had kept his long period of fasting, he was able to "see God's heavenly kingdom." Abū Sulaymān recommended fasting as a means of making prayer powerful and irresistible: "If you wish for anything in this world or the next, go hungry first and then pray for whatever you desire."[103]

Between their periods of fasting the Sufis could permit themselves the freedom to enjoy the good gifts of God to an extent which would have offended the ascetics of an earlier era considerably. There was a custom dating back to the time of the desert fathers, that when one met one's spiritual friends, one was allowed to indulge in a somewhat better meal. The Sufis considered it not only permissible but praiseworthy to do so, and to eat with pleasure when invited to such a meal. One day, Ma'rūf had been invited to a banquet, and a large number of delicious dishes had been brought to the table. A hermit who was part of the company looked with disapproval at the way in which Ma'rūf piled food on his plate and asked him repeatedly: "But do you not see how much you are eating?" Finally Ma'rūf said: "I have not asked for any delicacies. I would be content with a few half-ripe dates. But I am a servant who is ruled by his master: I eat what he gives me and sit down in the place to which he shows me."[104] Among the brethren joyful extravagance was permitted. On one occasion Ar-Rūdhbārī bought several loads of sugar and commanded a confectioner to make a castle of marzipan with towers, spires, and halls with many-coloured pillars. Then he invited his fellow-Sufis to demolish and plunder the structure.[105] Thus the Sufis, in contrast to the more narrow-minded ascetics, practiced what we might perhaps call 'gospel freedom'.

Chapter III

Solitude and Fellowship: The Believer and the World

When Dhū'n-Nūn was asked to describe "the pious ones who are concerned for their souls," he answered in his picturesque language: "They are people driven away from their homes by worry and anxiety. Sorrow is rooted deep in their souls. Their anxious thoughts seek God and their hearts fly with longing to meet him. Fear lays them low in the bed of sickness, and distress butchers them with the knife of punishment. Their plentiful weeping makes their heart's blood burst from them, and their spirits perish out of bitter sorrow for their Friend's sake. Their food is dry herbs and their drink is pure water. They rejoice in the words of the Merciful One and bewail their sins before Him with sorrowful voices like doves. They seek refuge in deserts and mountain gorges. They keep watch over the evening star, as it goes to its rest. With struggle and effort they endure the hours of the night watch. To flee from their fellow men is the innermost desire of their hearts."[1]

A current of religious romanticism runs through classical Sufism. The Sufis were fond of using old-fashioned religious expressions and ideas, and depicted contemporary Sufi teachers as they imagined the pious ones of the past to have been: ascetics and hermits, worn out by fasting and wakefulness, removed from people and living in the solitude of the desert and the mountains. Dhū'n-Nūn frequently tells how he himself has met these chosen ones and has been allowed to share their spiritual experiences. He states the place and the circumstances carefully: "I was travelling among the hills of Antioch. Then I caught sight of a girl, who seemed to be out of her mind."

"While I was walking one dark night in the hills near Jerusalem I happened to hear a sad voice and loud weeping."

"When I was travelling in the land of the Arabs, I found a man in a grove of oaks by the side of a spring of water."[2] Seemingly he would have us believe that he is describing actual experiences. This is hardly his intention, however. It is a literary form, part of a *genre* that was not his own invention. Probably originating in secular literature, in religious poetry it was certainly cultivated by an older contemporary of Dhū'n-Nūn, the famous grammarian and learned collector al-Aṣmaʿī (d. AH 216-AD 837). Al-Aṣmaʿī was also fond of choosing as a mouthpiece of mystical devotion some personality whom one would not expect to find in such a context: a young girl or a poor, illiterate Beduin, who appears in an unusual setting. He, too, ostensibly narrates a real event. Thus he describes an encounter with a young girl, who sings, while holding on to the curtain of the Kaʿba:

> O Lord, Thou alone givest safety and forgiveness,
> And Thy house gives merciful comfort to those who love Thee,
> To those who dream, on their bed of rest, of love's desire.

Al-Aṣmaʿī reproaches the girl for daring to speak about love's desire in such a holy place, whereupon he receives a lesson on the true nature of the love of God, which reduces him to silence.[3] In such poetry, being a framework of prose with lyrical insertions in verse, Dhū'n-Nūn loves to depict his romantic ascetic ideal.

Dhū'n-Nūn certainly had travelled widely to meet brethren and kindred souls in the spiritual life, but he would hardly have met them wandering about in the deserts or mountains. In actual fact the famous Sufi teachers of the third century AH lived at home, surrounded by numerous disciples and throngs of visitors from near and far. In theory they would very well have embraced holy poverty and given up their everyday occupations. Thanks to the flood of gifts from disciples or wealthy patrons, they were able to lead comfortable lives. Periodically they devoted themselves, as we have seen, to fasting and other spiritual exercises; but there was hardly room for a strictly regulated life of asceticism, once they had reached an acknowledged position of spiritual authority. All their spare time would then have been occupied by religious instruction, which many Sufis transmitted sitting on a cathedra in their lecture room, exactly like other famous traditionalists, while the disciples took notes diligently. What was dictated might be traditions from the Prophet—Sufism possessed its own rich store of such traditions—or statements of pious men in the past, or words of wisdom from the teacher's personal experience. The Sufis regarded with severity those unbelieving scholars who spent all their time collecting knowledge but did not care to apply it in their lives. Therefore it was a matter of common decency for the Sufi to avoid appearing himself as a learned authority. "I should like to ask you about a saying of Ibn Adham," someone said to Bishr. "Do not do it," was Bishr's reply. "Ibn Adham spoke and acted accordingly. You speak, but you do not act."[4] It is said about Junayd that, facing death, he arranged that all the notes taken of his words and sayings should be buried with him. He explained: "I will not go to meet God, having left behind my own words, while men turn their backs on the words of God's Apostle."[5] Fortunately his disciples did not follow this directive. The greater part of our knowledge of earlier Sufism springs from these very notebooks.

On the whole, a famous Sufi teacher thus resembled a professor of theology exercising his teaching function rather than a shaggy hermit. This is not in any way as an accusation that the Sufis' teachings were not lived out. On the contrary, their great achievement was this very fact of having transcended the one-sidedness and negativity of earlier ascetic religion and having reshaped it into devotional piety with positive aims and goals. By this process of accommodation of monastic religion to society in general, the Sufis in actual fact preserved the core of its seriousness and religious fervor as a spiritual power and source of inspiration for Islam.

Religious conservatism, which among the Sufis expresses itself in a romantic enthusiasm for the ideals and forms of a past age, may however initially make it difficult for us to discover how radically the situation had changed. The point at which this is most clearly noticeable is perhaps in the matter of social attitudes, the relationship between the individual and the community. The old ascetics were asocial, on principle. "Shun people as you would flee from a lion,"[6] is one frequently recurring saying. This is not only a matter of fleeing from evil, worldly-minded people, but from people in general. The really pious man should be a true recluse, inaccessible, aggressive and surly even towards his friends. Dāwūd aṭ-Ṭāʾī was as fearful of human beings as any wild animal. A man who had come all the way from Samarkand to see him, had to sit outside his door for three days without meeting him. For it was only when the call to prayer sounded that he left his house; and as soon as the *imām* had spoken his "Amen" he rushed out of the mosque with giant strides and disappeared through his own door. Not even his friend Fuḍayl was allowed to meet him. Fuḍayl stood outside the door; Dāwūd sat inside weeping, but would not open. Previously Dāwūd had in fact received visitors. But they had arrived in such great numbers and caused him so much trouble that he decided never to see anyone again.[7] Ar-Rabī' [ibn Khaytham] never left his house at all. One day when he was sitting in his porch, one of the enemies of the faithful had thrown a stone at him, hitting his forehead. Ar-Rabī' wiped the blood from his forehead, saying: "May God forgive him. He was not aiming at me." Nevertheless he regarded this as a warning and never, from that moment on, left his house, until he was carried out of it after his death.[8]

The Sufis, too, praised that blessed solitude in which nothing separates the believing soul from God. "God said to Moses: 'Be like a solitary bird who eats what grows in the treetops and drinks the clear water. When dusk falls, it seeks refuge in some cave, intimately close to me and far from the disobedient."

"The people who know God are the wild beasts of God on the earth. They show no affection for any human being."[10]

"The ascetics are strangers in this world. Those who know God are strangers also in the next world."[11]

Not even the concern for the spiritual wellbeing of others justifies us in leaving that solitude which is more precious than anything else for the peace of our souls and the purity of our hearts. It sounds like incredibly crass religious egotism, when Dārānī explains: "It does not harm the one who will be saved, that the lost one falls into perdition. On the day of judgment each one is responsible only for himself."[12] Aḥmad ibn 'Aṣim is reputed to have said: "Devote yourself to pious works, as if there were only yourself on earth and only God in heaven."[13] It is significant that this maxim closely follows a well-known saying by an Egyptian monk, Abba Alonis: "If a man does not think: 'Only God and myself exist in the world,' he cannot gain peace."[14] Fuḍayl kept to the old rule that one should be surly and dismissive even to one's spiritual brethren. One day he was sitting in the mosque in Mecca, when a brother came looking for him. Fuḍayl asked curtly: "Why have you come?"

"I have come to see you in private."

"No, by God! Do you really only want me to put on airs for you and you for me, and that I lie to you and you to me? Either you leave me, or I shall leave you."[15] And he used to say: "It is a clear sign of weakness in a man's intelligence, that he has many friends."[16]

This pretended negativity obviously in no way corresponded to the practices or the actual attitude of the Sufis. The mystical experience, like any other experience that enriches the heart and fills it with happiness, bursts through all the seals of silence. One cannot suppress one's joy. Incessant observation of one's own inner life brings with it a need for an intimate exchange of common experiences and mutual comparisons. The mystic experiences the ineffable, *to arrēton*; the experience arouses a flood of words. He therefore stands in exceedingly great need of fellowship. It is not very helpful that the ascetic ideal he has inherited prescribes solitude. Sarī's words sound like a sigh from a sincere heart: "I have practised all kinds of ascesis except the renunciation of fellowship with people. I have not achieved that, and I will not be able to do so."[17]

But the mystic does not seek people in general; rather he seeks the elect, those who have true understanding, spiritual friends. Like pious churchgoers of our day he makes "retreats," not in order to be alone, but in order to share his solitude with those of like mind. It is not the congregation, not the association, nor the organization, but the brotherhood, the spiritual circle of friends which provides an adequate form of fellowship within mysticism. How many such circles in the history of Christian mysticism have called themselves simply "The Friends"? Spiritual fraternity is necessary as help and support in walking the mystical road. Spiritual friendship leads to growth in grace. Personal example speaks more clearly than words. "You possess all that is good if you have a pious friend."[18]

"You should seek the company of the one who, when you see him, makes you think of God; the one for whom you can feel respect in your innermost heart; the one whose word makes you grow in pious works and whose example arouses your desire to renounce the world; the one in whose presence you are incapable of disobeying God; the one who exhorts you with his actions, and not only with his words."[19]

But the believer finds himself in a difficult situation in a world and in an age that is evil. Ibn Adham describes it thus: "Be full of concern for people, but be wary of people, for you cannot avoid them." Unfortunately, however, not all human beings are fully human: "The humans (*al-nās*) have disappeared, apes (*al-nasnās*) remain."[20] Therefore the rule of Sufi fellowship is: "Show respect to your elders, maintain close friendship with your brethren, be a sincere counsellor to your juniors and do not consort with those who do not belong to your circle."[21]

Inside this circle there ought instead to exist a higher degree of intimate and trusting fellowship. In the Sufi fraternity there was what almost amounted to practical communism: A Sufi arrives at a brother's house in the latter's absence. He commands the members of the household to open the money-box and takes out of it what he needs, without any scruples. And his brother is far from irritated by the other's taking such a liberty; on the contrary, he is happy that he has shown such confidence in his friendship.[22] Dārānī reminisces: "I had a friend in Iraq, to whom I would turn if I found myself in difficulties. When I asked him: 'Give me a little money', he simply handed over his purse, and I took what I needed. One day, as usual, I said: 'I need some money.' Then he asked me: 'How much do you need?' From that moment I could no longer rejoice in having him as a brother."[23] Above all, the faithful should support one another spiritually: "Among themselves, brethren are like hands; the one washes the other."[24] Brotherhood demands unlimited honesty. "You should choose for a brother one whom you can tell all that God knows about you." And: "You should never trust a brother, until he tells you to your face that of which he disapproves in you."[25]

It is no coincidence that confession was first practiced in such brotherhoods of mystics. Basilius' monks were required each evening to open their hearts to one another and not to suppress any sins or faults. In more difficult cases they were allowed private confession before their leader. Every fourteen days Buddha's monks would celebrate a ritual of confession. The brethren sat down in a circle. The monastic rule was read aloud, and following each commandment each individual monk would quietly whisper in his neighbour's ear whatever he might have done to break that commandment. A form of confession was also practiced in the circles of Sufi brethren. It is said of Shāh al-Kirmānī that he ordered his disciples to reveal to him their secret thoughts. Then he treated each one with appropriate spiritual medicine, saying: "He is not wise who hides his illness from his physician."[26]

When he hears the sin of his brother, the believer should not judge and reject him, out of spiritual pride and self-satisfaction. Instead, he is obliged to help him to get rid of his sin. "A true brother in God is the one who does penance in your place, when you yourself commit a sin," says Abū Yazīd.[27] A moving story, which could easily have appeared in a legend of some Christian saint, is the following: "Once there were two brothers in God, one of whom happened to give in to sinful desire. He revealed it to the other, saying: 'I have committed a sin. If you no longer wish to continue as my brother, then sever our bond of brotherhood.' But the other one answered: 'I shall never break that bond with you on account of your sin.' Thereupon he made a pact with God that he would neither eat nor drink until God had forgiven his brother's sin."[28] Then God had to relent and forgive the sinner.

That familiar and beloved means of devotional expression, the language of Canaan, once it is learned by the believer, cannot easily be unlearned. The Sufis continued to use the old sayings concerning the blessings of solitude, the importance of shunning people, fleeing—as Ibn

Adham says—"to the desolate mountains, from hill to hill, to preserve one's faith." But they attached a special meaning to solitude. By it they meant spiritual solitude, that stillness before God which is lasting, living with God in one's heart and for Him in all one's doings, that separateness which one is able to retain even in the midst of a crowd. When Junayd was a young seeker after God, he wished to live in solitude, but his teacher, Muḥāsibī, wanted to prevent him from becoming a spiritual isolationist. Junayd complained that he took him away from the close fellowship with God in solitude, sending him out into the world and the people, among whom he felt a stranger. Muḥāsibī replied: "How often must I hear about your solitude? If I had half mankind around me, I would not feel drawn to them, and even if everyone were to disappear, I would not feel alone."[29]

Traditionally there is a limit, in orthodox Islam, to this social isolation, the right to live alone with one's devotion. The limit is drawn by the duty of participating in public worship. The surly and misanthropic recluse who lived in his own home as though it were a monastic cell, would still have to overcome his dislike of going out among people, when the call to prayer sounded, at least once a week, at the Friday noon prayer. Even in his old age a handicapped and sick man like Rabī' would not absent himself from the mosque under any circumstances. Broken with age and suffering from the effects of a stroke he would totter, supported by two men, to the public prayer. His friends exhorted him to conserve his strength: "God will probably look upon your prayer with pleasure, even if you say it at home." But he explained: "He who has heard the call of the *muezzin* must respond to the invitation, even if he has to crawl there or propel himself on his bottom."[30] The Sufis observed the same rule strictly. Participation in public prayer is not only a duty but a privilege. If a man has happened to neglect communal prayer, steps should be taken to examine his life. The neglect is probably a punishment which God Himself has laid upon him, for some evil that he has committed.[31]

Such deliberate seeking of the fellowship of believers has always been important. Regular participation in public worship turns the worshipper's thoughts to the values and standards of the community. However dear the intimate circle is to the believer in God, he must take care that he does not, out of pride over his supposed spirituality, despise the community at large and completely withdraw from his fellow human beings, who, even if they may not be believers in the fullest sense, still are called 'the faithful'. In pious pride, a man in talking to a Sufi regretted the fact that he had to spend his time with so many worldly people. He received the following healthy advice: "If you are so certain that you are better than they are, then avoid being together with them."[32] Junayd emphasizes that the friends of God do have duties even to those who remain outside the circle of faith. It is true that you should not live in close intimacy with people who draw you away from God, but neither should you completely isolate yourself from people in the world. The believer should reflect on his duty to teach, nurture, and intercede for his fellow men. "It is your duty to help sinners and to teach them to understand how one speaks to God. You should be the one sent by God for their salvation. This is the task of the learned and the calling of the wise. And of all men those dearest to God are they who are of greatest help to His people and who make the greatest effort to be useful to all created beings."[33] Loyalty to Muhammad's community, to the congregation of the faithful, is a duty often strongly emphasized by the Sufis.[34] "God will number among His chosen friends the one who intercedes for the community."

Innumerable definitions and interpretations have been given of the concept of *zuhd*, 'renunciation', as of other Sufi terms and expressions. Thus Ibn Adham reassures us that the duty of the ascetic is to refrain from that which is forbidden; that asceticism which gives religious merit is to abstain even from that which is permitted. But the ascesis that gives the soul security goes beyond this, to the avoidance of that, the status of which is uncertain.[35] According to Muḥāsibī the nature of his ascesis must depend on the level of spiritual development the believer has reached. If he is at the stage of fear, he will reject that which is forbidden out of fear of God's punishment, and will perhaps also be able to reach the point where he can abstain from that which is permitted, fearing that he will not be able properly to thank God for His gifts. At the stage of scrupulous piety one abandons all those things, the permissibility of which may be in some doubt. He who has reached the level of trusting in God, refrains from feeling anxiety and worrying about his means of livelihood. He who has reached even higher, to the love of God, abandons all worldly things, because they are of so little worth. Some even consider that one should be prepared to renounce even Paradise, since the idea of Paradise is a mere nothing compared with the contemplation of God. But at the highest level, that of perfect love of God, one becomes capable of renouncing even "the brethren, who prevent us from reflection upon God alone." That does not mean the severing of all human contacts, but the abandonment of any fellowship, if it should prove a hindrance to a life devoted totally to God.[36]

Like other varieties of mystical theology, Sufism uses formulas similar to these, though far more complicated, in its attempt to reduce the varied world of inner experiences to systematic order. Pious scholasticism of this kind is generally of minor interest. What is far more important in this context is to find a fixed point of comparison, in concepts which we recognize as familiar and illuminating. Perpetual reformulations that add other indeterminate factors make the problems more intricate, but they do not offer a solution. "There are many opinions concerning the nature of renunciation of the world," writes ad-Dārānī. "Some consider it to be the abandonment of all human fellowship; others say that it is the suppression of carnal desires; and yet others that it means to refrain from eating one's fill. All these opinions in the end amount to one and the same thing. But my view is that renunciation means setting aside everything which draws you away from God."[37] His words hit on the essential and most decisive fact: renunciation is to abstain from that which draws us away from God. Its purpose and aim must be God and the world to come. To deny oneself everything in this world simply in order to find peace of soul is not right renunciation.[38] Can that be right renunciation, then, which is done out of an oppressive sense of duty, in conflict with our own will, reluctantly and against constant inner resistance? The problem whether it is greater ethical perfection to act out of duty than out of inclination is not unknown to Islam, and many have taken up an extreme position in advocating the performance of duty for its own sake. They have made it ethically normative in cases of doubt always to choose to that which conflicts most strongly with one's own personal inclinations.[39] "If a man does not do any good than that which he abhors, he will not be rewarded for his good deeds, nor will he save himself from punishment through abstaining from those evil things."[40] Every step forward on the spiritual path has to be gained in a struggle with one's baser nature and selfish will. But the goal is to attain spontaneous and free dedication to that which is good. To paraphrase the matter in Christian terms, the perfected believer is no longer subject to Law, but to Grace. If one is truly to renounce the world for the sake of God, that renunciation must be a result of the free choice and inclination of one's heart; otherwise it is unacceptable to God. "There are two kinds of ascetics," says ad-Dārānī, "those who renounce the world and yet do not feel the joy of the next world, and those who in renouncing the world already taste the sweetness of the next."[41] Renunciation in itself is not sufficient. It cannot be genuine and true if it does not spring from a heart which has already chosen God above all else in the world. "He who abandons sin without tasting the sweetness of obedience, will soon relapse into sin, and he who abandons sin without tasting the sweetness of renunciation, is not safe from relapse."[42] Therefore, as Muḥāsibī also emphasizes, renuncication becomes perfect only when worldly things are of so little value to the believer that they simply no longer exist. Perfect asceticism is no longer to feel renunciation of the world to be renunciation. It is to "renounce one's renunciation."[43] The true ascetic has driven out of his heart both joy and sorrow over worldly things, so that he neither rejoices in nor regrets the loss of anything that is of this world, not caring if his own life is difficult or easy. However, holy indifference, apathy, the elimination of all emotions is not the mark of Sufi piety. It is rather a sense of freedom and joy, a positive and active attitude. "It is part of true renunciation that one should rejoice in one's poverty and see in it the great grace of God at work. One ought to fear that God might take it away and rejoice in poverty just as a rich man rejoices in his wealth and fears poverty. One should taste the sweetness of renunciation, so that God, who knows our hearts, knows that we really love lack more than surfiet, humiliation more than glory, solitude more than company."[44] Here we have an atmosphere different both from that of the Christian anchorites and the strict ascetics of the first century of Islam, with their grim and unrelenting struggle against the ever-present desires of the flesh.

The Sufi master who most clearly embodies this Franciscan ideal is Ibn Adham. In him one senses a peaceful joy, like that of the Buddhist monks, a feeling of infinite relief at having turned away from life in the world with all its cares, troubles, and complexities. He rejoices in the trouble-free life of the ascetic under the open skies of God in the same way as would a person in our day, who has left the stressful life of the city behind and for a few precious holiday weeks is allowed to return to the free and uncomplicated life of the countryside. We have a snapshot in a way not unlike an anecdote from the biography of some Cynic philosopher: "Ibrāhīm ibn Adham was observed on a hot day, dressed in a fur-lined mantle, with the fur on the outside. He lay on his back at the foot of a hill, stretching out his legs on the rocks. He said: 'Kings also search for peace, but they take the wrong road."[45] On another occasion he said: "If kings and princes only knew how happy we are! Throughout their lives they battle, sword in hand, to reach that carefree enjoyment of life which we possess."[46] One day he was out walking with a friend. "We came to a spot where there was fresh water and dry grass. Then Ibrāhīm said to me: 'Have you brought anything in your bag?'

'I brought a few morsels of bread.' I spread them out, and Ibrāhīm ate and invited me to share in the meal. Then he stretched out on his cloak, saying: 'How ignorant worldly people are about us! There is no one in the whole world who leads a happier life than we do.' Thereupon he asked me: 'Do you have a family?'

'Yes, I have a family.' It seems for an instant as though he did not notice my presence. But when he saw the expression on my face, he said:

'But perhaps a married man, with his anxieties and cares for his family, lives in a happier state than we do.'"[47] With this last remark we catch a glimpse of the tact and sensitivity he showed to his brethren, but also of his natural and unaffected humility. Otherwise the Muslim ascetic, like the Christian monk, is immensely proud of his victories and heroic feats in the struggle against the flesh and its desires. Ibrāhīm regarded the following of one's innermost inclinations as no cause whatever for pride. He lived in celibacy, but without despising the one who was married. A man asked him: 'Why do you not marry?' Ibrāhīm answered: 'What do you think of a man who disappoints his wife and falls short of her expectations?'

'That is something one should not do.'

'Well, now, if I should marry and my wife desire of me that which a woman desires from a man, what would then happen? I have no need of women.' He lived in the utmost simplicity, but declared: "I do not think that I deserve a reward because I have given up delicacies, for I have no desire for them. A mouthful of bread with coarse salt tastes better to me than a date which wasps have nibbled."[48]

According to legend Ibrāhīm was "a king's son from Khorasan," and a romantic story is told of his conversion during a hunt.[49] On the basis of this narrative scholars have speculated that the figure of Ibrāhīm has been patterned on the prince of the Sākya dynasty (Siddhartha Gautama, the Buddha) and have drawn far-fetched conclusions about Buddhist influences on Sufism. In fact Ibrāhīm was an Arab of the tribe of Banu 'Adl, and a member of a distinguished family. He tells the story himself: "My father was a devout man, and in Mecca there was born to him a son, Ibrāhīm. He wrapped the new-born child in the patched mantle of an ascetic, took him to pious men and said: 'Pray to God for him!' It would appear that some of those prayers have been heard."[50] That legend has made him a prince is probably due to the fact that he frequently compares ascetics to kings: "By Allah, we are kings and wealthy men."[51] It is true that the beggar monk is compared to a king in Buddhist tradition; but the probability that what we have here is a borrowing from the Indian legend is very remote indeed. The expression is also found in the records of the earlier ascetics. 'Abdallah ibn Mubārak said: "Verily, the learned are true people and the ascetics true kings."[52]

Otherwise, his life-style was the complete opposite of the Buddhist way of life. Although on rare occasions he might also ask for alms, as we have heard, devoting himself for a time entirely to meditation and spiritual exercises, he would as a rule make his living out of hard and honest work. He gathered firewood in the hills and at harvest-time he would work in the fields. If no other work was available, he would tend vineyards and gardens.[45] He is said to have used the income from his work in part to support his disciples, who occasionally took unfair advantage of his unsuspecting generosity.[54] He did not practice compassion in the Buddhist manner, by allowing his *metta* to radiate out over hardworking and suffering fellow men, himself being filled with meditative peace; he would do it by helping them in practical ways.[55] A friend of his told the following story: "One day when I was chopping wood and felt tired from the work, Ibrāhīm went past. 'Are you tired?' he asked.

'Yes I am.'

'Do you want to lend me an axe and leave the work to me?' Then he put the wood on his back, took the axe and went away. When I had been waiting for a while, the gate opened. Ibrāhīm tossed in the axe and the chopped firewood, closed the gate and left." When he had recited the evening prayer, he stopped in front of the houses and called out: "Who needs help with milling their grain?" A woman came carrying one basket of grain, and an old man came carrying another. Ibrāhīm sat down at his handmill and did not go to rest until he had ground all of it. "If one cannot show one's generosity towards people by giving them money, food and drink, one should do so by showing gentleness and kindness."[56]

Otherwise, in terms of a historically documented biography there is not a great deal that we know about Ibrāhīm. The material for our knowledge of him, like that of several other Sufi saints, is similar to that which forms part of our synoptic gospels. It consists of sayings, not infrequently formulated with the clarity and expressiveness of a proverb, or a brief edifying anecdotes, often ending with such a saying as its point of emphasis. The artless narrative on occasion changes suddenly to an obviously legendary style. And yet Ibrāhīm as a personal type has something of that integrity which speaks more strongly than all historical documents. We stand face to face with a personality, which, because of its obvious and particular individuality, can hardly be a piece of fiction.

It is to the credit of those men whom I have called the classical Sufis that they saved mystical and individualistic devotion from the fate of becoming a sect. In so doing, they also made Sufism acceptable to orthodox Muslim believers and helped introduce its rich spiritual life into the congregation of the faithful.

The motives which principally dominate Muslim ascetic piety from its point of departure in the Qur'an itself, are, as we have seen, without doubt religious. That which binds a person to the world, preventing him from seeking after God and living according to His will must be rejected and sacrificed just as soon as it becomes a hindrance. However, the world itself is not evil, nor are property and family life necessarily hindrances in the search for God. In the circles with which we have been concerned here, there are hardly any traces of that metaphysical dualism which governs Hellenistic mysticism and Christian monastic asceticism. There are however occasional traces of such a view, for instance when we find in the ascetics of the earliest centuries of Islam a degree of bitter hatred of and contempt for the world that would do credit to the monks of the Scete desert. When it came to inveighing against the world, of calling it names and finding ugly epithets for it, and of describing natural life as revoltingly and distastefully as possible, the ascetics of Islam were well able to compete even with the Buddhists. "The world is like the devil, whom God has created to be damned and eternally apart from Him, to be both tempter and tempted, to be both destroyer and destroyed." A grim ascetic of the old school gives his view of the world: "I saw the world as a corpse and the devil lying on top of it like a dog. And a voice from above said to him: 'You are a dog of my dogs and the world is a carcass which I have created as your portion. If anyone should fight with you for anything which is part of the world, I will give him into your power.'"

"The world is the wine of Satan. He who makes himself drunk from it, will not become sober again before he staggers and falls in death."

The world is a latrine. One goes to such a place only in absolute need.

"The world is a swine, and if we knew a more hideous name, we would use that to describe it."[57]

God himself, although He has created the world, only hates and despises it. "The whole world in God's eyes is not worth so much as a gnat's wing," and "since the day He created it, He has not condescended even to glance at it."[58]

The Sufis probably also at times joined in the lament over the wickedness of the world. But when the believer considers the fundamental religious motive for this hatred of the world he has to recognize that it is not really the world that is evil; rather it is our burning desire for the world, the fact that we set the world above all else. It is the hypocrisy of our faith, that although we say that we love God, still we want to remain in the world rather than to part with it that we might meet God. God has not intended that the believer should entirely lose those good things, the joy and happiness which the world can give. But He has forbidden us to seek the world before and above Himself. "God will give this world also to the one who strives to reach the next."[59] The ascetic's savage hatred of the world is excessive and fundamentally irrational. "The world is like a bride. He who loves her combs and decorates her hair. The ascetic blackens her face, tears her hair out and rends her clothes. But he who possesses the knowledge of God is completely absorbed in God and does not worry about her at all."[60] This attitude of holy *apatheia* is also that of Dārānī: "The true ascetic does not revile the world nor does he praise it. He does not look towards it. He does not rejoice when it comes to him, nor does he mourn when it leaves him."[61]

But Sufism does not remain fixed in this negative stance. The heritage from the Qur'an comes to the fore. No religion which maintains that the world has been created by God can fall into total hatred and contempt of the world. "This world," we read, "is a bridge which leads to the next world. Walk across the bridge, but do not settle on it."[62] Thus the world is still "the handmaiden of God"; it is in the world and through the world that we must practice that faith which will carry us to the future life. Yaḥyā ibn Mu'ādh stressed this point of view so strongly that he was accused of being enamored with the world. He explained his point of view thus: "How could I refrain from loving the world, wherein God has given me livelihood and nourishment, whereby I am able to preserve my earthly life, the life in and by which I can achieve that obedience to God which guides me to the next world?"[63] He went so far as to consider it not only permissible to have possessions, but was also of the opinion that in certain circumstances wealth might provide a better moral starting-point than poverty. Old-fashioned ascetics, disapproving strongly of this liberal opinion, narrated with malicious pleasure how Yaḥyā himself experienced the "blessing" of wealth. A rich patron had given him a princely gift of thirty thousand *dirham*. His pious friends warned him: "God will not allow you to benefit from these riches." And indeed he fell into the hands of bandits who robbed him of his money and all he possessed.[64]

How often do we find religious ascesis being condemned as the enemy of all genuine humanity, all culture and progress! Thackeray once wrote of Thomas a Kempis' book *The Imitation of Christ*:

> If the fundamental tenets of that book were to be realized, this earth would become the most miserable, the most dismal and the most unhappy place imaginable. No humanity, no love, no tender bonds betwen mother and child, no fruitful work, no thought and no science; only a collection of selfish beings creeping about, constantly avoiding one another, whimpering an eternal *miserere*.

In fact negativism has never been—nor was it in Thomas' case—the last word in mystical piety. "If your heart be right," he wrote, "then every created thing will become for you a mirror of life and a book of holy teaching."[65] The Sufis also discovered that when the love of God sets a person free from dependence on the world, new value and fresh beauty are discovered in earthly things themselves. "The world is God's treasure-house, and that which God hates is not part of the world which He has created. For every stone or clod of earth or tree in the world praise God."[66]

"All things smile at the friends of God, those who possess the knowledge, with lips that proclaim the power of their Lord."[67]

The Sufis' devotional contemplation of Nature shows an awareness of its beauty and greatness that is otherwise—except in the Qur'an—rare in the religious literature of Islam. The Sufi master addresses his disciples: "When summer is coming the anemones burst into blossom and the trees spring into leaf. That is a good time to be travelling. Begin your wanderings at that time. For when the heart has long been immersed in the sea of meditation, our vision is obscured; but when we look at the fresh spring growth, the spirit of life returns to us."[68] Dhū'n-Nūn is a true poet, filled with touching happiness at the beauty of created things. "My God, whenever I listen to the voices of the animals, to the wind in the trees and the song of the birds; whenever I enjoy the coolness of shade, listen to howling storm and raging thunder, in all this I find a testimony to Thy goodness."[69] Tagore describes in his book *Glimpses of Bengal*[70] how, one evening on a river voyage, he saw the evening sky reflected in the quiet water. Then, suddenly, a large fish jumped close to the surface, and the mirror of the water was broken into a pattern of a thousand glittering circles: "A greeting from Him, whose nature is beauty." Curiously enough, Dhū'n-Nūn used an almost identical motif. In a prose poem, characteristic of his style, he narrates: "While I was walking on the river shore one night, I saw a girl in a coarse woollen cloak, her hair dishevelled. Her heart was filled with love of the Almighty, as she walked by the troubled waters of the river. While she was walking thus, she saw a fish shoot out of the water with a splash and flick its tail towards the sky. Then she cried out and said: 'All lonely beings remember Thee in their loneliness. The fish in the running water give praises for the hope they have in Thee; and the waves of the mighty ocean join hands in veneration of Thy majesty. The wild beasts of the desert rejoice in Thy love."[71] One day, when he stood by the seashore looking at the sky and the sea, he was heard to whisper: "How mighty, how exalted are ye two! But mightier still is your Lord."[72]

To the devout Sufi 'the world' is thus a concept which is, in the final analysis, religiously determined. What the world is, its value or worthlessness, is determined solely in terms of our relationship with God. Hence that peculiar ambiguity in the believer's attitude towards the world, which is familiar to us also from Christian literature. The world is at one and the same time evil and good, opposed to God and yet God's property. Even a Sufi author may declare: "It is out of the question for your heart to live in two worlds at once. If you have two hearts, then give one of them to this world and the other to the next. But if you have only one heart, then give it to that world which gives you lasting joy and permanent bliss." And then, in the same breath, he continues: "To leave the world is not to abstain from property, wife and children, but to act in obedience to God and to set the things of God above those of the world, both in what you use of the things of the world and in what you renounce. Obedience to God makes the world good. Therefore do not blame the world, blame yourself, if you do not use it in the right way. The world is God's property. If property falls into the hands of a dishonest man, it will be the cause of his downfall. If the property falls into the hands of a trustworthy man, it will become a means of honour and success. But the property in itself carries neither merit not guilt. The merit or guilt is yours. Everything depends on how you use it."[73] These are thoughts which might well be heard also in a Christian sermon on God and Mammon.

Finally, the religious motive also provides an opportunity for an ethically more profound view of the importance of ascesis and a corrective against excessive ascetic practices. A disciple once told Dārānī: "I envy the children of Israel."

Dārānī asked: "Why is that?"

The disciple replied: "Because of those three or four hundred years that they were allowed to live. For in those days they could pursue their acts of piety until they became dry like worn-out waterskins and bent like archways."

"Can you imagine nothing more important than that? No, in God's name, He does not require of us that our skin should dry up and stick to our bones. He requires the intentions of an honest heart in all our dealings with Him. He who is honest to God in this way for ten days, will achieve in that time as much as another man would during his whole lifetime."[74]

The great Sufi teachers were sufficiently knowledgeable about the spiritual life to understand that irrational and excessive hatred often betrays a secret and suppressed love. Excessive hatred of the world is suspect: "There are fools who practise renunciation out of hypocrisy and who desire to gain the good things of this world through pretended ascesis. They are the ones who believe that ascesis consists of denouncing the world, eating swill, dressing in wool, speaking ill of the wealthy and praising the poor."[75]

The extent to which the Sufis finally succeeded in overcoming hatred of the world and the individualistic isolationism of mysticism, and in feeling at one with the community of the faithful in every good and commendable effort, becomes clear in a prayer by Junayd.[76] This is remarkable, among other things, because in some ways it is reminiscent of the Christian Church's prayer of general intercession. It begins by praising God and praying for every spiritual blessing upon the intercessor himself. Thereupon he continues to pray for his fellow men, dead and living: "Turn Thy goodness and mercy toward all faithful men and women who have departed this life in Thy true faith. Be Thou a protector, guardian and defender to them and to us. Forgive the living the evil which they have done and receive their penance. Have mercy upon the transgressors, help the oppressed, heal the sick. Allow us and them to turn to Thee in sincere repentance, such as is pleasing in Thy sight. Be Thou, O God, a protector, guardian, defender and helper to those who fight in Thy holy war. Give them a mighty victory over their enemies. Let fortune turn against their opponents, shed their blood and let them fall prey to our brethren, the faithful. Prosper the rulers and their subjects. To those whom Thou hast set in authority over the faithful give support and lasting joy. Prosper their lives and the lives of those over whom they rule. Show them grace, goodness and mercy and bestow lasting joy upon us and them. Prevent the shedding of blood, let discord and insurrection come to an end and protect us from severe trials. In Thy mercy Thou hast promised us this, Thou who art all-knowing and all-powerful. Grant that we may never see the faithful of Islam draw their swords against one another or any dissension reign among the believers. Instead unite them in obedience to Thee and in all those things which bring them closer to Thee. O God, we pray that Thou wouldst lead us to glory and not to humiliation, that Thou wouldst raise us up and not debase us, that Thou wouldst be for us and not against us. Unify for us the course of things, those matters of the earth which are to be a means for us to fulfill our obedience to Thee, and a help in reaching agreement with Thy will; and those things of the next world which are the highest goal of our desire. In Thy providence send us that which is dearest and most pleasing to Thee and which best helps to bring us closer to Thee, O Thou who hearest the voice of all people and knowest that which is hidden, Thou Lord of the heavens."

I hope that it will not seem to be an exaggeration if I say that here we find an ethos which appears familiar to us, indubitably more familiar than strange. One might call Junayd's general intercession a classical example of the convergence of religious development.

Chapter IV

The Life of the Soul

Church meetings and conferences nowadays [the 1940s] often gather around a theme which is usually formulated as "nurturing the spiritual life." That is where one may learn to participate in congregational worship, to strengthen one's individual life of faith through reading, prayer, and meditation, and to practice the art of corporate prayer in the liturgical offices. And because the nurture of the spiritual life is best learned through personal example, one is recommended periodically to make "retreats" under experienced leadership. Where Christian revivalism had only a simple call, an appeal, one now finds a complete order, a method. We see how church-centered religious devotion is about to take the important step from spontaneous to systematically practiced religion. If spontaneous religion does not interest itself greatly in devotional method, this is due to the fact that in this type of religion the fundamental religious experience comes as a gift from above, full of inner strength and compelling activity which, irresistibly, takes possession of the individual. Our own action, that which we ourselves are to do or undertake, plays so small a part in this process, that the individual aspect is almost forgotten. It is quite another matter when the experience does not appear spontaneously, when it has to be sought out and called forth by appropriate exercises and methods. Exercise and method are characteristic of mystical religion, but one might also say that spiritual exercises themselves tend to reshape faith into religion of a mystical type.

The art of spiritual exercises cannot be learned on one's own. Its method cannot be absorbed like other areas of knowledge, but has to be observed and lived out by personal example. The first stage of the *via mystica* is therefore, in Islam as elsewhere, that of the disciple, the disciple in search of his master. The young man who feels called to walk 'the way of the poor', who is a *murīd*, a seeker, first has to find an acknowledged spiritual tutor. He should be a man who teaches not only by precept but also through practice, a man the mere observation of whom facilitates the living of the devotional life.

Convention required that the master should be reluctant and discouraging, and the disciple humble, eager, and intense. The sheikh had to make it understood that it was a severe trial of his devout humility to accept a role as leader and master of others. One had to fear everything, thought Ma'rūf, even one's circle of disciples. For the Prophet had said: "Discipleship implies a temptation for the one being followed, and a humiliation for those who follow."[1] It is salutary for the disciple, too, that the sincerity of his intentions should be tested. A certain young man sought to become a disciple of Abū Ḥafṣ, but he sent him away with severe words, saying: "Do not ever come to my classroom." The young man, however, was undeterred by the master's rudeness. He walked out backwards, without turning his back, out of respect for the great man. Thereupon he dug a hollow in the ground outside his house and determined to sit there until the master himself ordered him to leave. Faced with such humility, Abū Ḥafṣ capitulated and received him, and in time the young man became his favorite disciple.[2]

Under the continued schooling of the sheikh, the beginner had to learn two things above all: obedience and humility. In order to cure him of all feelings of self-importance, Junayd sent the son of a high-ranking man, one of the Caliph's chief administrators and governor of a province, to go begging every day in the market-place, until one day nobody gave him anything. "Now you see that you have no worth in the eyes of men", Junayd said.[3] Above all the beginner had to learn to wait, in humility and patience, for the day when the master found him worthy of being initiated into the deeper truth. Any conceited display of learning was severely punished. A man who had a very high opinion of himself and his own learning happened to hear that Dhū'n-Nūn knew the greatest Name of God and travelled from Mecca to Egypt in order to learn it. Dhū'n-Nūn did not like his looks and did not receive him with his customary graciousness. The stranger was however able to gain respect by involving himself in a disputation with a theologian to the point where the latter could no longer reply. From that moment the master honored him and paid him more attention than his other disciples. When one year had passed he asked Dhū'n-Nūn to teach him the secret Name. But he gave no reply. One day, six months later, Dhū'n-Nūn sent the man to a friend in Fustat with a bowl, lidded and wrapped in a napkin. And now the unhappy adept himself takes up the story: "When I came to the bridge between Gizeh and Fustat I thought: Dhū'n-Nūn is sending a gift to his friend, but the bowl is strangely light. I must have a look and see what it contains. I unwrapped the napkin and lifted the lid. Then a rat jumped out of the bowl and ran away. I became angry and thought: Dhū'n-Nūn is mocking me, and I returned, quite furious. As soon as Dhū'n-Nūn saw me, he realized what had happened and said with a smile: 'You fool, I entrusted you with a rat, and you deceived me. How could I trust you with the greatest Name of God? Get out of here, I do not want to see you again.'"[4]

Unfortunately we do not know a great deal about the day-to-day fellowship between masters and disciples during the earliest period. Occasionally they seem to have lived together as a brotherhood with a certain degree of common ownership. It was not thought proper if a 'seeker' spoke of someone's property and called it his own.[5] Ibrāhīm ibn Adham made it a condition, when he received someone as his disciple, that he should do every kind of work and give the brethren an equal share in all his property.[6] Otherwise it is said of Ibrāhīm that he supported his disciples through his own work. They were allowed to devote their days to fasting and other exercises, and when the sheikh returned home he first cooked their meal and then commenced his devotional discourse. This probably means that the master himself also submitted to the rule of pious communism.

Strict discipline reigned in these spiritual schools. Junayd went to visit Abū Ḥafṣ when the latter had moved to Iraq. He found his disciples standing in rows in front of him to do his bidding, and not a single one of them mistook his duty. Then Junayd said: "You have trained your disciples as a king trains his servants."[7] The period of discipleship lasted for one and sometimes for several years. But the spiritual dependence upon the teacher lasted for the remainder of the disciple's lifetime and it occasionally happened that the former disciple refused to teach the way, as long as his master was still alive.

A number of Sufi teachers presupposed that theological studies, mainly studies of the tradition, had preceded the seeking of spiritual guidance. Originally the ascetics had shown little respect for theological knowledge. The glory of learning was, rather, one of those worldly things which had to be renounced. Bishr buried seventeen boxes full of books in which he had written down traditions from the Prophet which he had heard. He was reproached for showing such lack of respect for the tradition, but he answered: "My ego desires to tell these traditions, and therefore I do not do so. If it were the case that I would rather not tell them, then I would. When someone says: "So-and-So has told me'"—thus placing his own name first in the long line of famous and holy men which leads through the ages back to the Prophet himself—"then he thinks: 'Move over to give me room!' This is nothing but worldly pride."[8] To pour scorn on the self-esteeming men of learning is something that the devout enjoy doing. It is typical of the secularized scholar that "he talks a great deal, likes his books to become famous and is angered when someone contradicts his opinions."[9] This characterization of professorial arrogance is valid for all time.

Otherwise two accusations above all head the list of crimes committed by the unbelieving men of learning. They gather knowledge, but they do not put this knowledge into practice in their lives; and they sell their knowledge for money. Especially severe criticism is directed towards the poor reciters of the Qur'an, those who earn their living by reciting, or rather chanting long passages out of the holy book at family celebrations, funerals and on various other occasions. They are people who incur guilt by the demeaning occupation of making a living from their religion. Among the mystics of the most severe school of observance, 'reciter of the Qur'an' becomes a pejorative term. These 'reciters' are judged in the same way as the free religious movements have always judged the paid ministry, the members of which live off their religion. If they are generous and less strict in their renunciation of the world, it is said of them that "they play with the world like children playing with marbles." If on the other hand they are strict ascetics, that is nothing but hypocrisy, in order to gain so much greater respect and income. "Flies on a dungheap are a more beautiful sight than the reciters of the Qur'an by great men's gates."[10] And in the believer's ears their recitals sound "more abominable than singing or lute-playing."[11]

However, the attitude of the Sufis toward theological learning was not as negative as one might think, on reading these severe indictments. All those individuals who appear in these pages were extremely faithful to the Sunna. Some of them, like Junayd and Muḥāsibī, were highly educated theologians, while others, like Dhū'n-Nūn and Yaḥyā ibn Mu'ādh, even demonstrated a certain degree of literary education. The

Sufis' criticism was only directed towards secular learning. They maintained, as a matter of fact, that one should start out with the study of tradition, and only afterwards embark upon spiritual exercises. This is the right and praiseworthy path: first to gather knowledge and then to put that knowledge into practice.

Thus knowledge has value. But the seeker has not come to his master in order to gather knowledge previously gleaned from the mouths of the traditionists or from their books. He does not seek knowledge, *'ilm*, but insight, *ma'rifa*, that kind of knowledge which is not learned by rote but experienced: not a burden which is carried as objectively as a donkey would carry books, [cf. Sura 62:5] but the innermost possession of the soul.

The one who has been initiated into the secrets of the faith is often simply called, in various religions, 'he who knows', that is, the one who knows more than ordinary people, possesses a knowledge which is not accessible by ordinary means. In this pregnant sense the Celtic prophet and sacrificial priest was called *druid*, and the Arabic poet who receives his inspiration through the *jinns* is called *shā'ir* . The holy and power-filled songs of the *rishis* are simply *veda*, knowledge. The classical example of insight in this sense is, of course, the *gnōsis* of Hellenistic mysticism and related Christian schools of thought. When the Sufi mystic is frequently called *'ārif*, simply 'the one who knows', and the dedicated community of the Sufis is termed *ahl al-ma'rifa*, 'the people of the knowledge', it is indeed very tempting to render this technical term by 'gnostic', or 'gnosis'. This has often happened, and I myself have done so in the past. However, it is undoubtedly an incorrect use of the term and might lead to a misconception of the essence and central message of classical Sufism.

Gnosis is not traditional, empirical or speculative knowledge in the usual sense. It stems from an interior illumination or revelation, and is gained by new power, a form of visionary insight which can be gained only through mystical initiation. Its content is other than that of common religious knowledge. It opens up fresh insights, for example into the origin of the world, the hierarchy of divine powers and the hidden nature of man.

Sufism also acknowledges transcendental insight which is given through direct divine illumination. Dhū'n-Nūn met a man who walked about barefooted in the desert wilderness, speaking confusing words about the sufferings of love and their cure, a cure which in fact only increases the illness. When he greeted the man, he answered: "Peace be also with you, Dhū'n-Nūn"

"So you know my name already. How are you able to have such clear insight?"

"It is not I who know. It is He who illuminates my heart, so that I am able to know who you are without having seen you."[12]

But such knowledge is not divine knowledge, *ma'rifa*. It is true that it, too, is the knowledge of a special kind, a *charisma* given by God himself. But in reality it does not have a different content from the usual faith experience. It has a different color, a new luminosity, an inner creative power. The difference is rather that between truth, merely acquired by study, and truth that has been really experienced, between dead and living faith. According to Dārānī the one who possesses knowledge has one advantage over others: "When he is asleep on his pallet God reveals to him that which He does not reveal when he rises to pray."[13] Here one might be tempted to think that we are dealing with a type of supernatural gnosis, secretly transmitted. But if one were to examine more closely the way in which Dārānī describes the one who possesses divine knowledge, one would find characteristics which do not fit into Gnosticism: "If the works of the believer, when he has attained the knowledge of God, remain the same as before, he walks according to his own desires. He who truly knows God, does not leave his prayer after two prostrations, before he has tasted their sweetness."[14] It is this interior joy, or bliss, which henceforth characterizes his works of piety. He no longer practices them out of compelling duty, but in the freedom of the spirit. His personality has a totally different atmosphere and aura. "Serving God through ascesis—that is like breathing vinegar and mustard. Possessing divine knowledge—that is like the scent of musk and ambergris."[15] In the same spirit it is said: "Those who know God in truth, their prayer is different from other people's and their innermost concern differs from that of others."[16]

The road to this higher knowledge is in fact the same one that leads to true faith and genuine love of God. "Knowledge of God is attained through obedience to Him and obedience is attained through God Himself."[17] Knowledge of God does not consist in pretentious theosophical insight. "He who possesses the knowledge of God is always the most humble of all people, because at every moment is the closest to God," Dhū'n-Nūn said.[18] All wordy protestations of extraordinary experiences are suspect. If one possesses the knowlege of God, one shows it by reverence for Him, not by attempting to describe that knowledge.

Knowing God is not only a great joy but also a nonparalleled responsibility. "The one who knows God can never feel lasting joy or enduring sorrow over earthly things. He is like a man who is seated on a throne, wearing a crown of glory. But above his head there is suspended a sword, hanging by a hair, and by the gate two beasts are prowling, on the loose, so that at every moment he is threatened with destruction. What could such a man rejoice in or sorrow over?"[20] That this knowledge of God does not have a new content, but essentially signifies a deeper, personal assimilation, an experience of the truth about God, Junayd expresses in more theological language: "The knowledge of the chosen is identical to that of ordinary people, because its object is one and the same. This object is limitless. How would knowledge be able to grasp Him, whom thought cannot reach, understanding cannot comprehend, intellect cannot conceive and to whom vision cannot give an image? Ordinary believers are at the first stage of knowledge. This means believing in God as One, denying that He has any equal, and having faith in His Book and the commandments and injunctions contained therein. The highest stage, that of the chosen ones, by contrast, means steadfast adherence to God and His truth, fearing Him at every moment, choosing Him above all His creation and shunning all those things which do not bring us closer to Him. The knowledge which the chosen ones possess above ordinary people is the powerful insight they have in their hearts concerning God's great power and majesty, His generosity, magnanimity and goodness."[21]

One's sense of religious nuances is very poorly developed if one does not immediately recognize that here we encounter a completely different spirit, a world far different than that of Gnosticism. The humility, the profound sense of responsibility and the moral seriousness are diametrically opposite to the self-importance and pretentions of the Gnostic, as well as his naive rejoicing in fantastic speculation, which no one is able to take seriously. If one were to compare Sufi knowledge of God with any other concept, one would rather choose insight such as it is described in the Gospel of John: "And this is eternal life, that they know Thee the only true God. . . ." (John 17:3).

"How curious it is that people should force their way across rivers an through deserts to reach the Ka'ba, the house of God, and to the sacred precinct in order to see there the footsteps of His prophets Abraham and Muhammad. But they do not care to penetrate the desert of the self and its desires in order to reach the heart and there find the traces of their Lord."[22] Sa'dūn sang, in the burial-ground at Basra:

> You search for knowledge far and near,
> But lo, its source is by your side.[23]

In the heart, in the world of inner experience, is where the mystic looks for the footsteps of God. That is where he hopes to find the secret of knowlege. But in contemplating this inner experience we do not enter a world at rest, a world that is static and therefore graspable. Modern psychologists have a great deal to say about this transitory character of the psyche, about the stream of consciousness which is in constant flux and can never be fixed, as a state of mind in a certain phase or a certain function. The Sufis, too, have described the inner life, in almost the same words but with a different meaning. "The inner experiences ['states', *aḥwāl*] are like flashes of lightning. Their permanence is only a suggestion of the lower soul."[24] This is how it is, and how it should be. The life of the soul, if it is really lived, must always be moving forward: there is something lacking in the one who is the same today as he was yesterday. For yesterday he was in a certain spiritual state and his striving was directed toward growth in that grace. If he has today reached that level of growth and rests content with it and does not aim for further growth, then an interruption in his striving has occurred, and he will not be able to sustain his existing level. This momentary character of experience also means that the believer can never describe the level of spirituality at which he finds himself at any given moment; he is able to describe it only when he has passed beyond it in his development.[25] Stagnation in the life of the soul is thus a sign of spiritual complacency and death. "The righteous man is changed forty times in a day, but the hypocrite remains in the same state for forty years."[26]

The life of the soul is thus in a constant state of flux. However, it is not like the movement of water in a fountain, whose cascades rise and fall in an eternally changing pattern, but always rising from the same point and falling towards the same surface. It is like the movement of water in a river, flowing steadily towards its goal. It is characteristic of all true mysticism that the constantly varying experiences form a chain, an ascending road, a *scala mystica.* Also within Sufism the believer is constantly striving to be able to grasp the rapid flashes of transitory experiences (*aḥwāl*) each as a new phase of a certain stage (*maqām*) on this road. The conversations between the seekers and their masters are largely concerned with these levels of spiritual achievement. Often a travelling brother who has reached spiritual maturity will join in the discussion; or the sayings of recognized mystical authorities will be quoted. For instance, a disciple inquires about that level which is called 'resting in the will of God'. The master explains what that signifies, how and from what point this level is attained and where it leads. In Sufi circles levels of spirituality are discussed with greater personal interest than protocol rank in a group of court functionaries. Progress and advancement on the road is not always to be understood in a temporal sense, but equally in an objective, conceptual sense. A Christian, similarly, has not left the spiritual stage of repentance because he has made progress in his spiritual development, even if repentance, objectively and ideally, precedes the stage of sanctification.

Junayd once formulated a very sensible basic rule: "That teacher is wise who, in describing spiritual states, goes to the utmost limit of economy and precision, and who is able to do so, because the experience which he depicts is present and clear in his mind."[27] It is a rule which the adepts of mysticism have so very rarely made an effort to follow. On the contrary, their descriptions of the degrees and stages of the spiritual life are characterized by extensive wordiness, a spiritual logorrhea, which often makes the study of mystical literature a somewhat tedious process for the uninitiated. In all justice we have to acknowledge that the classical Sufis often grasped the art of saying a great deal in a few words. Their sayings frequently have a concise, gnomic form and are ingeniously epigrammatic. It is, on the other hand, not always easy to grasp their real meaning.

I dare not try your patience with a detailed discussion of Sufi attempts at interpretation and systematization of inner experience. Permit me however to mention a couple of instances of sequential ordering of the spiritual stages. Dhū'n-Nūn enumerates: faith, fear, reverence, obedience, hope, love, passion, intimacy with God.[28] On another occasion he explains the highest levels as being: confusion, poverty of the soul, union with God. "Thereupon all the wisdom of the wise is lost in amazement."[29]

It is immediately obvious that there are very striking differences between the various chains. Sufism in effect knows no such clear and logical ordering of the mystical stages as does Christian mysticism, for instance in St. Theresa and St. John of the Cross; still less does it have a psychologically stringent and clearly thought-out directive concerning the inner path of salvation such as we find in Buddhism. This is without doubt due to the dominant role of the idea of God in Islam. The activity of God, His intervention, is perceived everywhere. The degrees or stages of the spiritual life are not steps which man is to take and prepare for carefully and methodically; primarily they are experiences of grace, which God gives and bestows upon man in His unfathomable liberality. They signify not a *scala mystica* but an order of grace.

This is the fundamental reason why the Sufi mystics do not have the same feeling of freedom and individual achievement *vis-à-vis* their inner experience as do other mystics. God is the first and the last. Everything depends on God's actions in us. One has to take care that the individual experience does not come between man and his God. Abū Yazīd explained: "I was separated from God for thirty years, and what kept me apart from Him was my own reflection upon Him."[32]

"The penitent is kept apart from God by his penitence, the ascetic by his acts of renunciation, the one who loves by his own inner experience. But the one who has reached union, nothing can separate from God."[33]

Thus we must be careful that our own spiritual experiences do not become the basis of our hope, usurping the place that belongs to God alone. Dhū'n-Nūn exhorts us: "Seek your support in God in your inner experiences; but do not seek in your inner experiences a support beside God."[34] This is something that Carl Olof Rosenius might also have said.[35]

Another characteristic of the earliest Sufi mysticism is probably connected with this powerful sense of God's activity. This is the comparatively limited role played in Sufism by rules and techniques designed deliberately to produce ecstatic states. As I have pointed out above, ascetic practices, above all fasting, served this aim, among others. Prayer was certainly also very effective as such a technique, in the way it was practiced in Islam, with its precise physical movements, genuflections and prostrations. It is frequently said about a mystic that he would faint with emotion during his nightly prayers. Even in the Qur'an there is mention of the nocturnal exercise called *dhikr*, which, together with the dance, has seemed to latter-day Western observers to be among the most characteristic traits of the cult of the Dervishes. *Dhikr* consists of perpetual repetition of the Name of God or brief doxologies. In prayer and *dhikr* the rosary is used as a devotional aid. One day someone noticed a rosary in the Sufi master Junayd's hand. "Do you, in your elevated position, take a rosary in your hand?" the person asked. But Junayd said: "I do not want to abandon the way in which I came to God."[36] During *dhikr* ecstasy might break forth in wild, uncontrolled screams. One of Junayd's disciples was in the habit of crying out, when he listened to *dhikr*. But Junayd, who loved sobriety and control, said: "If you do that once more, you may no longer be my disciple." Then he controlled himself so severely that beads of perspiration emerged at the base of every hair - but he did not cry out. Finally, one day, he was suffocated by his inner emotion: "His heart broke and his soul passed away."[37]

It is a striking fact that meditation (*tafakkur*) seemingly played a fairly limited part in Sufism. Curiously enough, when it is mentioned, it is often as having been practiced by the early ascetics. Ḥasan al-Baṣrī declared: "One hour's meditation is better than waking all night."[38] Among Sufis who practiced meditation, special mention is made of Ibn Adham. One of his disciples was asked if Ibrāhīm prayed a great deal.

He replied: "No, but he used to sit meditating at night."[39] Dāwūd aṭ-Ṭā'i, one moonlit night, was sitting so deep in meditation "on the kingdoms of heaven and earth" that he accidentally fell into his neighbor's garden.[40] Ma'rūf was also among those who meditated frequently. A disciple narrates: "We were often together with Ma'rūf at his house. He used to sit engrossed in meditation for a long while; thereupon he woke up and said: "'My God, I seek my refuge in Thee.' We thought nothing more remarkable in him than this meditation."[41] As subjects for meditation are noted: the wonders of creation, our good and evil deeds, God's goodness towards us and His greatness. We are given an approximate idea of the nature of Sufi meditation, when we read Ghazālī's instructions.[42] According to Ghazālī, meditation is primarily an act of the intellect. In contrast to *dhikr*, the simple "repetition of a thought until it is firmly fixed in the heart," meditation is a discursive process of thought: "By linking two truths one arrives at the third, which will provide new knowledge, an insight which one did not previously possess."

I have not been able to find any similar description or manual of meditation in the Sufi classics. In my opinion this is due to meditation in fact having been practiced in connection with the reading of the Qur'an, and especially during the nightly prayers. "Meditation in prayer is better than meditation without prayer," it is said.[43] It is notable that the recital of texts from the Qur'an was part of both free and liturgical prayer. We hear frequently that a Sufi reading the Qur'an at night was gripped by one single verse and remained immersed in deep reflection for hours, profoundly moved by its *ḥalāwa*, its sweet delight. Thus Dārānī could remain in contemplation of five verses for the whole night, "and if I had not ceased to reflect upon them, I would never have passed beyond them. It often happens that one comes to a verse that completely overwhelms one's mind."[44]

One spiritual exercise particularly characteristic of Sufism consists of trying to induce religious ecstasy through singing, sometimes with musical accompaniment, or recitation—it is well known that the difference between solemn recitation and singing is not very great in the Orient. As early as the second century AH mention was being made of particularly gifted female singers who knew how to recite the Qur'an in an extremely moving manner. 'Aun ibn 'Abdallāh had a woman slave, Bashīra, who read the Qur'an "with melodies." One day he asked her: "Read to my brethren," and she read "with a mournfully drawn-out voice." Then the men pulled their turbans off their heads and burst into tears. 'Aun was offered one thousand *dīnārs* for Bashīra's beautiful voice. But he declared: "No one else is going to own you! Go, you are free before the face of God!"[45] The marked preference for a sorrowful and lachrymose tone of voice is noteworthy. Mas'ar ibn Kidām (d. AH 155-AD 772) preferred, when hearing the Qur'an recited, to listen to "a cooing, sorrowful voice."[46] Arabic zoologists compare the sound of the dove with the voice of "a woman who is reciting the Qur'an."[47] The melancholy, slow and half-sobbing tone of voice which is often heard when listening to the daily poetry reading at noon on Radio Sweden, would have suited the oriental ideal admirably.

Spiritual song or recital was however a novel phenomenon which orthodox Muslims at first found extremely shocking. Dārānī is surely referring to these pious recitals, when he says: "Whatever else you may doubt, do not doubt the fact that your nightly meetings are an objectionable innovation."[48] One can understand his reservations, because just as people generally preferred listening to female singers in secular musical entertainments, so they would seem frequently to have had the same preference at the spiritual recitals of the Sufis. In addition the spiritual songs appear for the most part to have been purely secular love poems which were applied to spiritual conditions, in the same way as Christian mystics would use the wedding poems of the Song of Songs. No wonder, then, that Ḥasan al-Baṣrī strongly disapproved of such a questionable form of spiritual entertainment. Even Ibn Adham was of the opinion that "song brings forth hypocrisy in one's heart."[49]

By the ninth century, however, these spiritual recitals had become a permanent feature of Sufi devotional life. In a story about Dhū'n-Nūn we hear about the proceedings at such a gathering: "When Dhū'n-Nūn came to Baghdad, a group of Sufis gathered around him. They brought a reciter and asked that he might be allowed to recite something. Permission was given, and the man declaimed:

> A small amount of longing pains me so;
> Longing, in full flame, hurts so much more.
> You waken in my breast that strong desire
> That almost makes a pagan of my soul.
> Lament the one who suffers such distress!
> The free man smiles, and yet desires to weep.

Dhū'n-Nūn stood up, overcome by emotion, and then he fell down, his face touching the ground.[50] However, he had evidently also heard female singers perform similar spiritual love songs. On such occasions, he had felt himself transported to that heavenly bridal chamber of which the Qur'an speaks, and had imagined hearing the soft voices of *houris*: "The songs express the intimacy of a secret chamber. They are performed with the deepest feeling by chaste women's voices."[51]

When listening to evocative singing and music, the Oriental is gripped by a degree of emotion, the force of which is hardly imaginable to the cooler, northern temperament. When Abū Ḥafṣ' disciples heard devotional songs, they tore their garments, overcome by weeping. Someone asked if such behavior could be called dignified, but the master retorted: "What does a drowning man do? He grasps hold of anything which he believes might save him."[52] The mystic who listened to singing drowned in a sea of love. Not even Junayd, sober and severe as he was, denied himself this spiritual pleasure. But he controlled himself and showed no emotion. Despite his inward turmoil, he kept his peace. When someone wondered how he alone could remain cold and unmoved, he answered with a quotation from the Qur'an: "Thou shalt see the mountains, that thou supposest fixed, passing by like clouds" (Sura 27:90).[53]

Strange as it may seem, Junayd did not like to hear the Qur'an recited by a sentimental singing voice. This he felt to be inappropriate to the divine seriousness of the holy scripture. People asked him: "Why are your disciples not moved, when they listen to the Qur'an?" He answered: "What in the Qur'an should move them, here in this world? The Qur'an is truth and it has come from the Truth, and it does not belong together with anything human. Every letter in it makes a demand of the individual, a demand which he cannot escape, until he has fulfilled it before God. But when the disciples listen to the Qur'an in the next world, coming directly from Him who has spoken it, then it will move their hearts."

"But how is it that they are moved by poetry?"

"That is because this is something that they themselves have created; it is the language of lovers."[54]

Junayd must have had reservations about the rightness of singing, but in a dream he was reassured by the Prophet himself, who explained: "Every night that you have practiced such things, have I been present among you. But begin by reading the Qur'an and end with it."[55] Junayd made it a rule, however, not to arrange these devotional song recitals for larger groups, but only together with his closest fellow-believers and his family. He also prescribed that only "the people of his house"—in this case surely his own women slaves—should perform the songs.[56]

In Paradise the devotional song will sound one day, in a more exalted choir, for the enjoyment of the faithful. When the redeemed are allowed to listen to the celestial concert, "every tree in Paradise will be rose-colored."[57] Dhū'n-Nūn describes how God gives grace to the blessed by letting them "listen to spiritual voices" and hear David read his Psalms. If you could only hear David! A high lectern is brought out, selected from among all the lecterns of Paradise, and David is given permission to ascent it. All those living in Paradise, everyone from the Prophets to the Saints, the "spiritual ones" and "those close by" are listening. Then David begins to read the Psalms, and the hearts of all are stilled by his beautiful, sustained reading, his gentle voice and exquisite diction. Time is forgotten, hearts are close to bursting with joy and the faces of all are wreathed in smiles. The wide vault of heaven answers David, and its closed chambers are opened. Thereupon David raises his voice to make their joy perfect, and when they hear him, "those who live in the highest heights" emerge from their lofty chambers, and *houris* answer him from behind the draperies of the rooms, singing seductively. The seats in front of the lectern shake, currents of air move lightly and the trees tremble. Voices answer one another, and the song begins to sound in alternation. The King of Heaven gives increased powers of comprehension to the blessed, that their bliss may be perfected. And if God had not ordained that they should remain for ever in Paradise, "they would die of happiness."[58] During the spiritual song recitals the mystic is allowed to experience a foretaste of this ineffable delight.

Dancing, too, has been used as a means of producing ecstasy, as sometimes happened in early Christian mysticism. When Yaḥyā ibn Mu'ādh was asked if dancing might be permissible, he answered:

> In dance we move upon the earth,
> Thy hidden being thus rules us.
> There is no sin in such dancing
> For one who is charmed by Thy love.
> Each step that we take while dancing
> Is therefore a walk in Thy valleys.[59]

When the believer keeps watch in the stillness of the night, praying and reading, he may experience a joy and inner fullness which secular souls cannot grasp. "If night did not exist," Dārānī said, "I should not care to live on earth. I do not wish to live merely in order to dig ditches and plant trees. To the people of obedience their disquiet is a greater pleasure than is merriment to the carefree men of the world."[60] The believer may occasionally, during his reading of the Holy Book, come upon a verse which "totally confounds his understanding." He enters a state of ecstatic rapture. As early as the second century AH we find stories about believers who fall into ecstasy, lie in their prayer niches far from the things of the earth and do not answer when spoken to.[61] When Muslim ibn Yāsir stood praying, a firebrand fell down beside him, but he did not notice anything, until the fire had already been put out. When he prayed at his home, he told his family and servants to talk to one another, if they wanted to, because, he said: "I do not notice your conversation."[62] The nature of the ecstatic state "cannot be described. It is a secret between God and the believing soul."[63] It can be grasped and communicated only through direct experience: "Those who sense something of the presence of God only do so, when they themselves are lost in this presence, and I who tell you about it must myself be in the same presence."[64]

The Sufi mystics are remarkably reticent in their descriptions of ecstasy, giving only the merest hints of those marvellous things they have seen and experienced in their moments of rapture. The expressive form given to their ecstatic experiences is usually the description of a journey of the soul upwards into the heavenly spheres or down into subterranean worlds. This is a familiar image, and one which is encountered among various peoples throughout the world, being apparently based on similar psychical experiences. Hellenistic mysticism, and the Christian mysticism which derives from it, plays an essential part here. The Sufis probably came to know it through the narratives of the Ascension of the Prophet, which attracted such an amount of biblical and Christian legendary material. There is an early story of Ibn Adham, in which a disciple marvels at the fact that the holy man spent all night lying on his side, without getting up even once to pray. But Ibn Adham answered him: "I have spent all night travelling, now through the gardens of Paradise, now in the chasms of hell. Can you call that sleeping?"[65] Dārānī depicts the ascension of the soul as the final stage on the mystic path: "When souls are confirmed in the conquest of sin, they wander through the heavenly kingdom and return with wonderful wisdom, such as no learned scholar can attain through his learning."[66]

The image of the ascension of the soul recurs with particular frequency in Dhū'n-Nūn. "The souls of the perfect ones ascend from the tips of the angels' wings. They descend among the ranks of those who praise God and seek refuge in the houses of those who glorify Him. They hold fast to the veil of Omnipotence and commune with their Lord, so that with their inward eyes they perceive the power of the Almighty and His great Kingdom. Thus their hearts return, with firm insight into Thy divinity."[67] It is characteristic that what the soul gains from ecstasy is not new knowledge, but a deeper knowledge of God. In effect, Dhū'n-Nūn uses the ascension of the soul as an image of mystical union with God. Properly speaking, he does not describe ecstatic experience or vision, but its religious value and consequences. One of the most frequent epithets he applies to the perfected saints is: "those whose bodies are present on earth but whose spirits wander in the heavens, in the Kingdom of God." The formula is part of the devotional language of both Hellenistic and Christian mysticism. "Without leaving the earth he is in heaven," is

Poimandres' description of the spiritual man (*pneumatikós*). "Their visible bodies walk on the earth, but all their thoughts rest in the Lord," writes Aphraates.[68]

Dhū'n-Nūn uses expressions which remind us even more strongly of the familiar imagery of monastic mysticism: "I beseech Thee . . . to make me one of those whose spirits freely roam the heavens and whose innermost thoughts are totally intent on conquering their desires, so that they reach the garden of bliss, gather its nourishing fruits and drink from the cup of Love, immerse themselves in the sea of joy and seek shade in the abode of grace. O God, make me one of those who drink from the cup of faithfulness, which gives them patience in long periods of affliction, so that their hearts reach Thy Kingdom and fly between the veils surrounding the mysteries of Thy kingly rule, and their spirits attain that wind-cooled shade where the lovers dwell, those who come to the garden of peace, to the place of Omnipotence and the eternal dwellings."[69] According to Christian monastic legend the perfected spiritual man can ascend to the highest heaven whenever he wishes to do so. As proof he brings back fruits which he has picked in Paradise.

In this instance, Sufism has thus come close to the conceptual world of gnostic theosophy, but has not passed beyond the borderline. Not even Abū Yazīd, who stands closest to the gnostic mystical type, has crossed that threshold. He describes a vision of celestial and subterranean worlds, but he does not do so in order to impart his new spiritual insight. Yaḥyā ibn Mu'ādh said that he once saw Abū Yazīd in visionary trance during the whole of the time from evening prayer to dawn. "He was crouching on the ball of his foot, with his heel and instep raised from the ground, with his chin sunk upon his breast, staring in front of him without blinking. At dawn he knelt and remained kneeling for a long time. Then he sat up, saying: 'O God, there are those who seek after Thee, and Thou givest them the ability to walk on water or to walk in the air, and they are content with this. I beseech Thee: keep me from becoming such a man. There are those who seek after Thee and Thou givest them the gift of travelling in a moment across the whole earth, and they are content with this. I beseech Thee: keep me from becoming such a man. And there are those who seek after Thee, and Thou givest them the hidden treasures of the earth, and they are content with this. I beseech Thee: keep me from becoming such a man.' In this way he enumerated some twenty kinds of miraculous gifts which God gives to those who love Him. Then he turned around and saw me and said: 'Yaḥyā?

I replied: 'Yes. Lord.'

'How long have you been here?'

'For a long time.' Then he fell silent. But I said: 'Lord, tell me something (of what you have experienced).'

'I shall tell you something that might be useful to you. God took me to the lower realms. He let me travel about in the kingdom under the earth and showed me soils and what is below them, as far down as the damp earth. Thereupon He took me to the highest sphere and let me travel about the heavens, and I was allowed to see the gardens of Paradise and approach close to the Throne. Thereupon He set me before Him and said: 'Ask for something that thou hast seen, and I will give it to thee.' I replied: 'O Lord, I have seen nothing which I found to be so beautiful that I should like to ask Thee for it.' Then the Lord said: 'Thou art truly my servant! Thou servest me with a sincere heart, for my own sake.'"[70] Nothing in heaven or on earth, not even perfect knowledge, is greater than possessing God Himself.

Chapter V

GOD THE ONLY GOD

In one respect there is a striking dissimilarity between the Christian ascetics' world of ideas and that of their Muslim counterparts. The Christian hermit has to endure a permanent struggle against the devil and the armies of evil. Demons hover in their thousands around his solitary cell, watching his every action and thought and trying to disrupt his devotions. They appear in all manner of disguises: whether as a serious travelling brother who enters the cell on a visit, or even as an angel from heaven; whether as a wanton, painted and dressed-up city woman or as an Egyptian farmer's daughter in her light working clothes. Should the demons succeed in causing the hermit to fall into temptation, they then show themselves in their real, loathsome shapes and disappear, with loud peals of scornful laughter.

This picturesque ingredient is almost entirely absent from the pious narratives and legends of the Sufis. However, earlier ascetics on an occation experienced demoniacal temptations similar to those of the monks. Amīr ibn 'Abd Qays was among those who were particularly plagued by the Evil One, who would curl up in the shape of a snake in Amīr's place of prayer and leave an evil odor behind. Once, in the same guise, he crept in among his clothes. Another ascetic of the second century AH assures us that "around the believer Satan assembles hordes of devils, more numerous than Rabīʿa and Muḍar."[1] Naturally the Sufis, too, often speak of *Iblīs*, Satan.[2] He is the enemy of the soul above all others, the one who seeks to tempt and seduce the believer with his 'whispers', his evil promptings. When the believer does not refrain from that which is forbidden, "his heart falls under the power and sway of Satan."[3] Satan watches every human being carefully in order to find a weak point where an attack can be launched. "The Devil asks about every human being seven times a day. If he hears that someone has turned from sin and is penitent, he raises a shout that gathers together all his brood, from East to West. They say: 'What distresses you, Lord?'

'So-and-So has repented. How can I find a stratagem to lead him into perdition? Is there anyone among you who is a friend or relative of his?'

Then one of the devils in human form answers: 'Yes, I am.' Iblīs thus sends him to try to turn that man from the way of repentance."[4]

It is a curious idea that evil human beings are the intimate friends and the bodyguard of the Devil, in a similar way to warlocks and witches within Christian popular belief! The Devil breaks into the human heart, like a thief, in order to steal the individual's faith.[5] He exploits his or her self-satisfaction and wordly assurance. "When the believer becomes accustomed to doing good works, he begins to regard this habit as a trait of his own character, and thus regards these works as his own merit. But the Enemy, who lives in the individual's own home and has pathways within that person's body, like the blood flowing through the veins, is watching him, in his guile able to see everyone's hidden spiritual negligence. In that way Satan removes from him that which he would otherwise not be able to touch."[6]

It is a striking fact that the Devil is often mentioned in precisely those statements which show a degree of Christian influence. "Satan asks you every morning: 'What will you eat, what clothes will you wear, where are you going to live?' Answer him thus: 'My food will be death, my clothes the shroud, and my house the grave.'"[7]

"The friends of God are like fishermen who fish human beings out of the jaws of the Devil. Now, if a friend of God catches only one, during his whole lifetime, that is sufficient achievement in itself."[8]

Occasionally we also find stories about visions of the Devil. Junayd eagerly desired to see Iblīs, and eventually he was granted a vision of him, in the shape of an old man with such a terrible aspect that no one could bear to look upon him.[9] On another occasion the Devil was seen walking about stark naked in the middle of the market-place, eating a crust of bread. When Junayd asked if he were not ashamed to appear like that, the Devil replied: "Those people before whom one might have been ashamed, have disappeared nowadays."[10]

Otherwise the Satan of Islam is, like Luther's Devil, "ein melancholischer Geist." When he comes, wanting to make the believer depressed by his promptings, one should counter them in a positive spirit, "for nothing is as hateful to him as the believer's joy."[11] And it has to be remembered that temptation often follows the highest spiritual experiences: "The bliss of reflection upon God is accompanied by the bitterness of Satan's promptings."[12]

However, the devil actually plays a very limited part in the world of classical Sufi imagination. It is true that his name is never mentioned without immediately pronouncing a curse. But they never take him quite seriously. "What does the devil matter? If one disobeys him, he cannot do harm, and if one obeys him, he cannot be of help."[13] And Dārānī even explains: "Among all the beings that God has created there is none that I despise as much as Iblīs. Verily, if God Himself had not commanded me to pray for His protection against the Devil, I would not do it." He also regarded a human devil as worthy of greater fear than a supernatural demon.[14] And Rābi'a gave unforgettable expression to the Sufis' central attitude towards belief in the devil: "The love of God does not leave any room in me for hatred of the Devil."[15] There is only One who is worthy of fear and veneration, just as One alone is worthy of love and trust: God Himself. It is hardly a coincidence that even the Prophet himself, as the great intercessor and mediator, probably does not play a less important role anywhere in Islam than that which he has been given in classical Sufism.

It is well known that in his philosophy of religion Hegel describes the religions of the world as gradually escalating expressions of the finite spirit's conception of itself as absolute soul: the religion of suffering, the religion of mystery, the religion of utility, the religion of beauty, and so on. Islam he groups with Judaism as 'the religion of sublimity.' Had he known Islam in greater detail, he would surely have found profound theoretical reason for calling it the religion of seriousness, for that would be a most appropriate description. Cromwell's Puritanism appears almost frivolous compared to early Muslim asceticism. To laugh is sinful; games and jokes are an expression of the satanic element in human character. Rabī's little daughter asked her father: "May I go and play?" But he answered: "I have never found that God has ever been pleased with those who play."[16] A brother who laughs is warned: "Beware lest God calls you away at this very moment." It is probably not too farfetched to assume that the serious, reserved solemnity which is characteristic of the true Muslim even today, derives from this fundamental trait in Islam.

In this way one individual man's experience has shaped the thoughts, customs and way of life of a people and a culture for thousands of years. Muhammad had experienced God as the mighty king on the Day of Judgment. His earliest revelations with their terse, succinct verses breathe an incomparable atmosphere of intense emotion, reverence and fear. Before the Lord of the Day of Judgment, man is but a speck of dust; and dust in the very real sense is what man would like to become in order to avoid the immense responsibility of being human. As an old saying has it: "If a command were to come from my Lord, offering me the choice of being a man, with the possibility of going to Hell or Paradise, or turning into dust, I would choose the latter."[17]

God is the Lord, and man His slave. "If I did not fear that I would be thought only to be drawing attention to myself, I would command that I be laid in my grave with my hands tied, so that I could be returned into the hands of my Lord like an escaped slave." This terrified reverence for God was felt also by the Sufis. When Ma'rūf had to recite the call to prayer, he shook and trembled out of reverence and fear of God. And when he came to the words: "I affirm that there is no God but Allah," the hairs of his eyebrows and beard stood on end with fear, so that it seemed as though he would not be able to complete the call.[18] Even Abū Yazīd, who felt himself lifted in mystic rapture to the throne of God, and felt his human self merge into His divine being, nevertheless harbored the same fearful reverence for God. Once a man was standing behind him when he was saying the noon prayer. He observed that when Abū Yazīd wanted to lift his hands and pronounce the words: "God is great," he could not do it, being in such awe of the name of God. His whole frame was trembling so much that his bones could be heard protesting.[19] He wandered about restlessly for a whole night along the city walls of Bisṭām, wanting to say: "There is no God but God," but his reverence for the Name of God overwhelmed him so completely that he was not able to pronounce it. When dawn broke he descended from the city wall, and his urine had changed to blood.[20]

With no less reason, however, Islam may be called "the religion of sublimity." The Qur'an describes the greatness, wisdom, and goodness of God as revealed in His creation, in verses that show indubitable traces of biblical models, perhaps especially Psalm 104. We have seen that this subject was a main theme of Sufi meditation. Among Sufi poets Dhū'n-Nūn in particular adopted, enriched, and deepened the idea that Creation reveals the manifold riches of God's own being: "When Thou didst begin the wonderful act of creation in the hidden world of Thy foreknowledge, then the glory and beauty of Thy face was revealed in all its wealth in the great and marvellous order in the manifold expressions of Thy being."[21]

The omnipotence of God, His greatness, and His sublimity, above all that human thought can grasp and words express, Dhū'n-Nūn has celebrated in a magnificent hymn of creation.[22] It is a remarkable document, for it demonstrates, with convincing clarity, that in Sufi piety God is far from being conceived only as that intangible correlate of mystical union, the sea of love, the river of light, the One without form or limit; but He is also seen as active in creation, even though His nature is incomprehensible and inaccessible to human thought. This hymn is of such importance that I feel compelled to quote *in extenso*:

> Thou art Most High, O Lord. No one in the world can know Thee.
> Thou yet knowest all beings, art able to grasp and see all things.
> None of our questions can reach Thee—why? whence? or whither?—
> Neither art Thou encompassed by any measure or limit.
> How could there be limits to Him, when no eye can see Him
> And He is like unto nothing that thought is able to reach?
> He, at the source of existence, made all things appear. He created
> All that exists, out of nothing. But he will always remain
> Constant for ever, in ages to come, the times that are changing
> When He so wills it. No decrease or increase is within Him;
> Constant remaining though earth and heaven were not, neither
> glimpse
> Of the world of being. All praise be to Him, who governs for
> ever!
> He grew not in power when life He bestowed on creation;
> He did not need its help to vanquish an enemy's power.
> All in Himself He possesses, and nothing is lacking in Him,
> While His creation is bound by the forces of change and endeavor.
> His withholding life from that He has not yet created
> Shows Him not powerless to hasten His work. He tires not
> To enclose all things that are hidden in His mighty Providence,
> He, whose omniscience holds every matter both present and future.
> All that exists must confess its anguish and need of assistance;
> He will give help to those who seek their support in Him.
> He knows each object, whatever its changing condition,
> Every thing that is born, and all that dies, being transient.
> Every secret He knows, which the heart would keep to itself;
> Nought that moves in the depth of the soul is hidden from Him.
> He inclines his ear to the words of all people; His eye sees
> Each tiny insect wending its way across rock-solid ground,
> Wandering clouds, every one, and pools drying out in the sun's
> warmth.

He is the first and the last, He is the Lord, One and Only.
For Him there exists nothing 'near', neither is anything 'distant'.
He is exalted and mighty, all-knowing and without end.
Eternal being He was and eternal will He continue.
He is above the doubter's thoughts and the scornful insults
From one who never accepted His acts of liberal mercy;
No words of praise, whatever your effort come close to His greatness.
No being on earth exists, whose song of praise can attain to Him;
Powerless it climbs at the last but to the rim of eternity.
Yet He is praised by the tongues of those who knowledge have gained.
Never a Lord thou wilt find other than Him [the Almighty].
Once He divided the light from the darkness that lay there and covered
The face of the waters, where waves surged and billows in foam roared upon them.
To the mass of the darkness high over the storm-wind its place He allotted,
On the waves of the ocean unsteady it floated. With power of creation
He established it firm in the rocks of the hills and He placed there,
Held fast in the mountains and stones of the earth, its powerful pillars.
The vault of the heavens He spread as a roof, and He built it
In seven-fold levels, alone He accomplished and made them.
His almighty power sustaining the heavens and weight of the earth.
Never the burden doth tire Him, fainteth He not nor is wearied.
Thousandfold made He with liberal hand all His works of creation,
Manifold beings in all their abundance by groups and by families
So He created. Then caused He His own nearest image to rise
In the midst of the creatures whose time on the earth must be brief.
Lo! hosts of angels eternally laud Him in meek adoration,
In time and eternity wearying not in their singing of praises!
Throughout all the ages four mighty ones stand at the foot of His throne.
One bears the form of a bull; eagle, man, lion the others;
Each prays for the beings, the likeness of whom each one carries
Amid all the creatures, for life in the mercy and peace of God.
He made the vault of the heavens, their hosts in each image celestial
That move through aetherial oceans and follow the paths of the Zodiac.
Some of the stars wander widely; others stand fixed in their stations;

Falling stars flame, created by God to hurl at
Rebellious satans, each one that boldly approaches His Paradise.
He who would stealthily move to listen more closely, encounters
The flaming fire of a star, watchful for ever on guard.
There clouds give birth to powerful storms, and soon is observed
How lightning flashes through pouring rain and showers of
hailstones.
The air becomes pure, and grants to the world with the freshness
of life
A promise of hope for the body and soul of all things created.
All things He has made, He has decreed must die. To no one is
granted
Either final escape or a refuge wherein shelter is found.
Death, though, shall die at the last: all things created shall
perish,
And none eternal remain save God the Almighty Himself.

The poem has many details that are of interest to the history of religions. The idea that the animals before the throne are intercessors each for their own species is ultimately Iranian in origin.[23] The thought that the angels are the "nearest image" (literally 'shadow images', *ashbāh*) of God seems utterly foreign and offensive in an Islamic setting. Above all, however, Dhū'n-Nūn's poem possesses real beauty and poetic grandeur. It would be to do no great injustice to Cleanthes, were we to compare this work to his famous *Hymn to Zeus.*

It may seem remarkable that Dhū'n-Nūn should so strongly emphasize the aspect of God as eternally inaccessible, one who cannot be reached by the eyes of mortals. It is Dhū'n-Nūn, we recall, who is always speaking of those perfected mystics whose bodies remain on earth while their spirits roam in the Kingdom of Heaven and penetrate even to the Throne of God. "He lifts the veil between them and Him, and they see with the eyes of their hearts what He has destined for them, although yet it is hidden."[24] Alas, ecstatic vision is only perception through the eyes of the heart. No actual and real vision of God is possible for mortals. "No one who has seen God can die, just as no one can see God and live (an earthly life). He who has seen God, his life is eternal, for He whom he has seen will remain in him."[25] The thought that visionary perception, *epopteia*, conveys divinity and immortality is a familiar one, coming from Hellenistic mysticism. But Dhū'n-Nūn wishes to emphasize at the same time that the blissful seeing, the *visio beatifica*, belongs to the future life. One cannot meet God as immediate reality, here, in this world. When Yaḥyā ibn Mu'ādh sings:

Blessed be Thou, O Almighty God of Heaven,
Great in glory and exalted in deeds,

My prayer to be granted a vision of Thee is my heart's joy.
How great will my joy be then, when that prayer is answered![26]

he cannot expect this fulfillment of prayer in this life. He himself explains: "If human understanding were indeed able to see, with the eye of faith the joy and the bliss of Paradise, souls would be transported and dissolved by their longing. And if the heart could attain the real object of its love, the Creator Himself, the bonds of being would burst, and souls, dazzled, would flee from their bodies to Him. Praise be to Him, who does not allow His creatures to comprehend all these things, but to occupy themselves with a description of them, instead of letting them grasp their true nature."[27] It is true that in his experience the believer encounters something which he perceives as a Being that actually exists; but that which he thus imagines himself meeting is merely his own idea of God: "God is not distant, so that one would have to search for Him, and He has no limit, so that one would be able to reach Him. The one who thinks in his search for God, that he has reached something that exists, he is deceived by this supposed existence. For that which exists is, in my opinion, only our knowledge of God. True knowledge of Him is gained only through His actions."[28]

Even were someone to penetrate so deeply into the knowledge of God that he knew the greatest Name of God, he would not have gained any real knowledge of Him. "There is no clear concept of what this Name truly signifies. The Name is only the ability of your heart to absorb His divinity."[29] It is the grace of God, that He has ordained it thus: "God allows His servant to taste the bliss of His presence, but for the sake of the servant's joy He keeps him away from the true reality of that presence."[30] But although reason cannot comprehend God, nevertheless He is not unknown to the believer. The expression "to see God" may be used to describe this knowledge by faith: "The nature of God is existence without limit and without immanence. One sees Him with one's eyes in His retribution, in His Lordship and power. He has hidden His innermost being from man, but leads man to Him through His signs. The heart knows Him, but sight does not reach Him. Believers see Him without comprehending Him or reaching the limit of His being."[31] From this enlightened point of view one is also able to accept sayings such as the following, by Ibn Adham: "One hundred and twenty times have I seen God and asked Him seventy questions. Four of them I have mentioned to people, and they disapproved of them; the others I have kept secret."

The ecstatic vision is joy and bliss, yet it is not ultimate certainty. There is something still higher. Therefore, when Dhū'n-Nūn was asked, on his deathbed: "Do you wish for anything?" he answered: "That I might come to know Him, for one single moment, before my death."[32] God is *to epekeina*, eternally transcendent, says Sahl: "For God there is nothing beyond, and beyond Him there is nothing, but for all that exists, He is that which is beyond."[33] Abū Yazīd himself is of the opinion that "knowledge of the innermost nature of truth is ignorance, and insight into the deepest reality of the knowledge of God is a crime."[34] This *docta ignorantia* is the only knowledge of God which is accessible to us. There is a saying ascribed to Abū Bakr—though with total disregard of what is historically possible—which says: "God has not provided any other way to knowledge of Him, than the inability to reach such knowledge."[35]

Direct knowledge of God is not possible, thought Junayd. He was asked whether the knowledge of God is empirical or rational. He replied: "We are able to know things in two ways: that which is present we know through our senses, and that which is absent we know through proof. Since God does not appear to our senses, we must learn to know Him through proof and searching. Only by proof do we get to know that which is hidden and the Hidden One."[36] 'Proof' in this context certainly does not mean rational proof, but the capacity of reason to conclude, from the evidence of God's activity, that He really exists. According to simple orthodoxy as expressed by Mālik ibn Anās, all people will see God with their eyes on the Day of Judgment.[37] For the Sufi mystics the *visio beatifica* in the next world is a gift of grace which God bestows upon His chosen saints and friends. Muḥāsibī renders his own understanding in the form of an alleged tradition from the Prophet John, son of Zachariah. "God said: 'John, if one of My servants loves Me and I know this of him, I shall become the ear by which he hears, the eye by which he sees, the tongue by which he speaks and the heart by which he understands. When this happens, I shall make the thought of others than myself hateful to him, bring him to constant reflection, keeping watch by night and thirsting by day. O John, I am the friend and confident of his heart, his highest desire and hope. He comes close to Me, and I to him; I hear his words and answer his prayer. Verily, by My Omnipotence and Glory, I shall raise him to a position which will be the envy of prophets and apostles. Thereupon I shall command a herald to proclaim: 'Behold the friend of God, His chosen and elect one among all His created beings. He has called him to visit Him, that he may heal his breast by gazing upon the merciful face of God.' When he comes to Me, the veils are lifted between Me and him, and he may look upon Me, freely."[38]

Muḥāsibī's disciple Junayd, on the other hand, could not contemplate receiving an actual vision of God even in the next world, not did he *want* to imagine such a thing: "If God should say to me: 'Behold Me,'

I should reply: 'I will not behold Thee.' Because in love the eye is other (than God) and alikes the jealousy of others. Eyes would prevent me from beholding Him. Since in this world I was wont to behold Him without the mediation of the eye, how should I use such mediation in the next world?"[39] The believer thus loves God without seeing Him. Indeed, it is as the Invisible God that he loves Him.

The celebrated revivalist preacher B. S. Taylor delighted in giving hell-fire sermons, since "God's particular blessing would attend them."[40] In a sermon given some time in the early twentieth century he declared that: "Hell has been burning for six thousand years, and it is re-filled every day. Where is it? About 120 miles from here. In which direction? Straight down, 120 miles deep in the bowels of the earth." It seemed to his terrified listeners that the earth might split apart at any moment, and red-hot flames burst out of the crevices. But the quotation might have been taken straight from one of Muhammad's sermons in Mecca. Islam arose out of a form of revival preaching, the main argument of which concerned judgment and the fear of hell. According to Ribot, there are two opposites which constitute the chief modes of religious feeling: fear, respect, and veneration on the one hand, and admiration, trust, and love on the other, or the sense of the divine as *tremendum* and as *fascinosum*, to use Rudolf Otto's terms. Of these opposites, in the Qur'an it is decidedly the former that is dominant. Devout is the man who fears. One should fear the sins one has committed, fear that the accumulated store of one's good deeds will not suffice, and that God, at the last, and without regard to our deeds, in His inscrutable counsel has decided to send us to hell. Islam, especially as it emerges in pre-Sufi asceticism, may, with every justification, be called a religion of fear.

And yet (is this a peculiar contradiction or an altogether natural phenomenon of reaction?) there is no religion to compare with Islam in having a powerful antidote to religious fear, nor is there any that has sold, at such low cost, the bliss of which the true believer dare hardly speak. According to an idea which is very popular, though hardly orthodox, the great Intercessor for all believers, the Prophet Muhammad, will be allowed to lead out of hell everyone who simply recites the creed of Islam, even if there is not a grain of living faith in his heart. In reality this does not signify a more confident religious hope. It is merely an opiate against a fear, which continues to be the dominant trait of the faith.

Among the Sufis, however, it is without doubt the positive mode of feeling that is dominant. But a religion nurtured and taught by the words of the Qur'an can never forget that the fear of God nonetheless is the beginning of faith. The Sufi mystic, too, knows by experience what the fear of hell is. "Often I imagine myself to be in hell with my head between two mountains of fire, and sometimes I seem to feel how I am thrown into hell and sink down into its depths. How could the world give any happiness to the one who feels like that?" asks Dārānī.[41] Another Sufi confesses: "I look at my nose twice every day, because I am afraid that my face may have turned black."[42] For one's face to have turned black, as though already charred in the eternal fire, is believed to be a mark of especially evil sinners, who are quite clearly destined for hell.

And yet there is something that one must fear even more than the flames of hell: "The fear of hell, compared to the fear of being separated from God, is like a drop of water over against a mighty ocean."[43] The love of God does not exclude fear: "True love is fear, for unbelievers love God too, but their love leads them to complacency. The love of believers, on the other hand, leads to fear."[44] The devout man must have a sense of fear. Ḥasan al-Baṣrī has described ideal piety in the spirit of the Qur'an: "Of all people the pious man is the one who performs works of the greatest devotion and who fears God most deeply. If he were to give a mountain of riches as alms, he would still not feel safe (from God's punishment), until he sees Him. The more he grows in righteousness and goodness, the more he will increase in fear, so that he says: 'I cannot be saved.'"[45] Among the Sufis, too, fear is one of the essential characteristics of piety. "He who does not fear that God will punish him, even for his greatest works, will perish."[46] Although one may have reached the highest stage on the road of perfection, it is necessary again and again to instil fear in one's heart with exercises belonging to the lowest level: the thought of death; of the graveyards where Munkar and Nakīr, the angels of punishment, torment the recently buried individual in his grave; of resurrection and judgment.[47]

But over against God's wrath there is His mercy; over against the God who judges there is the God who forgives. Therefore "the believer should fear God more than anyone else, and yet feel safer with God than with anyone else."[48] Every *sūra* in the Qur'an, every book, every letter and document begins: "In the name of God, the Merciful, the Compassionate." God shows mercy in the same way that a father is merciful towards his children. A Sufi once saw a man take his little son in his arms and kiss him. He said: "You love him greatly because you brought him forth. How much more will not God love him, He who has created him."[49] The believer "stands facing his sin and facing God's grace and does not know if he should first ask for the forgiveness of sins or give thanks for the grace of God."[50] At the exact moment when the soul cries out: 'Father, I have sinned,' that soul knows that the sin is forgiven and is able to approach the stern Judge with extraordinary boldness. A famous prayer by Dārānī, to which we have made reference earlier, says:

> Lord, if Thou wilt judge me by my secret thoughts,
> I will judge Thee by Thy divinity.
> If Thou wilt judge me by my sins,
> I will judge Thee by Thy grace.
> And even were I to be sent by Thee to hell,
> I would proclaim my love of Thee to those who dwell therein.[51]

God *desires* that the sinner should believe in His forgiveness. Nothing arouses God's wrath as much as the belief that any sin committed by a human being could be so grave as to be beyond the reach of His forgiveness.[52] "Worse than sin is to despair of God's mercy, and worse than committing wrong is to postpone repentance."[53] In their amazement at the incomprehensible depths of God's grace—that grace which reveals its power to save at the very moment of realizing that one has sinned—the Sufis exclaim, like one of the Fathers of the Early Church: "*O beata culpa*!" We find a hint of this idea as early as Ḥasan al-Baṣrī: "If the pious man commits a sin and repents, thereby he will only come closer to God. And though he sin yet again, his repentance will take him even closer to God."[54] The thought recurs fairly frequently in Sufi writers: "None of the acts of piety David practiced was as salutary to him as was his own sin. It filled him with fear, and caused him to eschew the world until he was united with his Lord."[55]

"Blessed are the sinners who repent, but the righteous man must take great care."[56] The *motif* recurs in a story about Ibn Adham, with an endearing hyperbole in truly Oriental style: One dark night, in rain and thunder, he was circumambulating the Ka'ba, all alone. When he arrived at the door, he prayed: "O my God, preserve me from ever sinning against Thee." Whereupon a voice from inside the Ka'ba answered: "O Ibrāhīm, you ask Me to preserve you from sin, and all My servants pray in like manner. Now if I were to hear your prayer, to whom could I then show My mercy and to whom would I grant My forgiveness?"[57] If all men were without sin, the God of forgiveness would be out of work! Dārānī even reaches the bold conclusion that it is better to have been first ensnared by the world and then to have turned and repented, than to have grown up from the beginning as a paragon of ascetic living. On one occasion the faithful were talking about a man who had grown up wearing the woollen cloak of the Sufis and eating bread baked in ashes. "I should have preferred," Dārānī said, "that he had been one of those who had first tasted the joys of the world and had thereafter abandoned them. For such a man is no longer deceived by the world. But one who has not yet tasted worldly joys, of him you cannot be certain that he will not lapse, once he has experienced them."[58]

The tension between these two basic factors, fear of God and His punishment on the one hand and the hope of His grace on the other, is the active element of faith, its living pulse. Sahl has expressed it in a profound statement: "Fear is a male element, hope is a female element. Out of the two there is born the deepest truth of faith."[59] Another Sufi expresses it more poetically: "Fear and hope are like the two wings of a bird. If they are in equilibrium, the bird itself will be in balance and its flight will be perfect."[60] Dhū'n-Nūn, it is true, was of the opinion that "fear must be stronger than hope. For if hope takes the upper hand, all is not well with the heart."[61] The majority, however, maintain that there ought to be a relation of equality between them.

That factor which will bring about an equilibrium between God's wrath and His grace, is repentance. Only the purely secularized religion which relies exclusively on the membership of Muhammad's community of grace, believes in salvation from perdition without repentance. Every orthodox Muslim knows that God requires repentance and that He will receive the repentant sinner. "God loves those who repent." [Sura 2:222] But the mystic's view of repentance penetrates to a deeper level. "Ordinary people repent of their sins. The chosen ones repent of their good works."[62] Even the very best acts that the human being performs are tainted with sin and therefore imperfect. Our repentance, too, however honest, is always imperfect. Right repentance, therefore, according to a frequently quoted Sufi saying, is "to repent of one's repentance."[63]

Repentance has to be total and must encompass the whole of our lives. And above all, it must not become a species of accomplishment on our part, by which we might earn the grace and forgiveness of God. Repentance must not intrude between us and God, so as to obscure the unconditional and sovereign liberty of grace. This thought is developed by Yūsuf ibn al-Ḥusayn [ar-Rāzī], a contemporary of Junayd, in the following, highly remarkable statement: "If penitence were to knock of my door, I would not let her in, if she came to rescue me from my Lord. And if honesty of heart and purity of intention both were my slaves, then I would sell them, because I am able to be without them. For if I live a hidden life with God, blessed by Him and received into His mercy, then I cannot regress by committing sins and doing wrong. And if I am rejected and deserted by Him, then no penitence nor honesty nor pure intention of mine can make me acceptable. For God has created me as a human being, without any deed or merit on my part; and without anyone having interceded on my behalf with Him; He has led me to that faith which is pleasing in His sight. Thus I should rather rely on His grace and goodness, than on my own imperfect acts and qualities. To relate His grace and goodness to our own actions shows very limited knowledge of

Him, who is generous and merciful."[64] This saying might certainly give rise to misunderstanding—as might similar hyper-Evangelical statements within Christianity when they claim that every deed which we consider that we should or can perform in order to gain God's grace is worthless and could even hinder and damage our salvation. The writer moves along a very narrow path indeed. However, his intention is surely not to argue that repentance is not a necessary step on the way of salvation; rather it is the positive one of emphasizing, with the acuity of a paradox, that "God unknown, He alone, calls my heart to be His own."[65]

If the essence of piety is found in the constant tension between the two poles—the fear of God's judgment and the hope of His mercy—can man then ever be certain of his salvation? The orthodox believers of the old school answered that question with a brusque No! First, how could a person ever be certain that he or she has right faith and right works? "Man has performed deeds which he regards as being good, but on the day of reckoning, when the scales are set up, he may perhaps find that they were evil. And if you have no other sin, you must remember that the secret idolatry of the heart is more difficult to discover than the tracks of an ant across bare rock."[66] Secondly, if a person were to feel certain that he really is so good and so perfect that he has earned paradise, then this would be a terrible presumptuousness. And he has already proved, by this very assumption, that he must rather be destined for hell. On one occasion people were talking, in the Prophet's presence, about a man who was exceptionally devout, and he received extravagant praise. Just then the man himself arrived. "His face was dripping with water from the lustration, he carried his sandals in his hand and his forehead still showed the marks of his having pressed it to the ground while praying. They whispered: 'That is the man we were talking about.' But the Prophet replied: 'I see a mark of the Devil in his face.' And when the man had sat down in the circle, the Prophet asked him: 'I adjure you by God that you answer me honestly. Did you not think, when you came to us: 'I am better than all the others'?' He answered: 'Yes.'"[67] Spiritual pride was that devil's mark of possession which the Prophet had seen in his face.

And finally: how can a human being know that God will make any allowances for all his or her pious merit and good works? In the end God does as He pleases. It is said that Muhammad was heard to pray: "O God, I beseech Thee to forgive the sins which I know and those that I do not know." Then his disciples asked him: "Do even you fear Judgment, you who are the Apostle of God?" He replied: "And why should I not fear? God holds the hearts of men between His fingers and turns them as He wishes." Many believers have been humble to the degree that they have not even dared to pray to God to be allowed to go to Paradise; for that might be presumption, as though one regarded oneself worthy of such a request being granted.

What, then, is the attitude of the mystics to the question about the assurance of salvation? All mysticism is a striving to attain direct union with the object of faith, to experience, feel, and see that to which faith aspires. Mystical experience itself is bliss and eternal life; it is the possession of God in one's heart. The Christian mystics of the school of Amalrich explained that he who knows God already possesses heaven, in the same way as one who has committed a mortal sin already carries hell within himself.[68] The mystics of Bamberg denied that there would be a resurrection at the end of time, since the true believer has already been raised to life eternal. The mystics of Islam have also walked the road that leads from faith to experience; they have been granted a spiritual vision of the heavenly kingdom and by faith have attained union with the soul's Beloved. In so doing, had they not gained even the assurance of not having to share the lot of the damned in hell?

The fundamental religious mood of Islam, that of awe before the Omnipotent Judge, is in fact so strong that even the mystics—with few exceptions—have not dared to feel certain of their salvation; at least they have not dared to express such a certainty. For it would of course be a misunderstanding if one were to assume that the believing Muslim could never be certain, in practice, and in the confidence of his heart and his faith, of God's forgiveness and of going to His Paradise. But to pronounce this assurance in words would be a mark of spiritual pride. It would be trespassing into the realm of the Unknowable God and His glory. Not even the most blissful spiritual experiences—no, not even visions and experiences of the joy of Heaven—must make man certain and secure before God. "If a man were allowed to enter a garden containing all manner of trees, and upon each tree there perched every variety of bird, and each one of them were singing in a human tongue: 'Peace be with thee, O beloved of God,' and if his heart then were content with this, he would be a prisoner of the self."[69] This we might call 'worldly assurance'. The fear of an unhappy end accompanies the believer in each secret thought and in his every movement. "How could I rejoice in my acts of devotion, when my sins flood over me, and how could I rejoice in hope, when the end is unknown to me?"[70] The question was put to another mystic: "'What is it that causes you constant inquietude?' He answered: 'Only the one fact that God has created me and that I nevertheless do not know for what destiny, whether for the joy of Paradise or the pains of Hell.'"[71]

Abū Yazīd himself, who speaks more boldly than anyone else about the union of the believer with God, confesses: "The situation of those who have the knowledge of God is like that of the damned in Hell. They neither live in it, nor do they die."[72] Between life and death, between fear and hope, that is where he feels himself to be, despite all his talk of ineffable joy and bliss. He once said: "Such is my joy when I fear Thee. Then what will my joy be like, on the day when I feel safe from Thee?"[72]

God is zealous. He jealously guards that secret of preordination which is to be revealed to man only when He himself pronounces it on His great Day of Judgment. He does not desire man to despair of the possibility of his attaining salvation. Neither does He want him to believe that he is already in possession of it. "Thus He leaves man wandering in the desert of choice and submerged in the ocean of uncertainty. The one who believes that he has already reached Him, He will separate from Him, and the one who believes himself to be separated from Him, He is only putting to the test. Thus one cannot altogether reach Him, nor can one escape from Him. He is the Inescapable God."[74] It is true that individual Sufis have been of the opinion that the sincerely devout believer has the right to be certain of God's forgiveness. It is said that Ḥātim al-Aṣamm asked a brother "How are you?" He replied confidently: "Saved, and with my sins forgiven." But Ḥātim disapproved of his over-confidence and said: "Salvation is found on the other side of the Chinvat bridge, and there is forgiveness in Paradise."[75] One day man must pass that bridge across the chasm of perdition, the bridge which is as narrow as a hair and sharp as a knife-edge. Only when he has reached the other side, can he say: 'I am saved.'

According to Calvin there is indeed a possibility of becoming certain that one is predestined for bliss. It becomes evident in one's way of living. If one does the works of the elect, then one is preordained for heaven. The Sufis have occasionally come close to the same idea. A young man asked Sarī: "'Master, does the servant know that his lord has accepted him in grace?' He answered: 'He does not know it.'

'Yes, (but) I know it.'

'And how can you know that?'

'When I see that God keeps me from committing sin and that He helps me to obey Him, then I know that He has accepted me.'"

But the Sufi masters judged such thoughts as marks of over-confidence and lack of understanding.[76] They could not regard their own actions with such bold assurance. On the contrary, when the true believer considers his own life, he is forced to conclude that he is predestined to perdition. Abū Ḥafṣ confessed: "For forty years now I have believed, fully and firmly, that God looks upon me with the eye of wrath. My actions indicate it."[77]

Chapter VI

TRUSTING AND LOVING GOD

"God is too great and elevated to be angered or pleased by anything that a mere insect such as man might venture to do. But He has looked with the eye of wrath upon certain individuals, even before He created them. Thereafter, when He allows them to be born into their earthly existence, He permits them to commit the acts of wrath and finally He consigns them to the dwellings of wrath. He has looked upon others with the eye of grace, even before He created them, and later, when He guides them into existence, He allows them to perform such acts as are pleasing in His sight and eventually He grants them a home in the dwellings of His grace."[1] Like all orthodox Muslims, the Sufis, too, take the view that God in His eternal precognition has elected certain individuals to eternal bliss and destined others to eternal perdition. It is the fundamental tenet of Islamic religion that God alone has unlimited power and unlimited freedom. The doctrine of man's free will is therefore the most serious heresy. "How terribly do the adherents of free will blaspheme against God! They believe of the devil that he is able to nullify the will of God.

They think that when they themselves want something, that is how it will be. But that which God wants, does not happen."[2]

When one seeks to demonstrate the impossibility inherent in the doctrine of predestination, one usually describes the fatal consequences which result from this doctrine. It must (it is argued) have a totally stultifying effect on man's will, moral effort and eagerness to work towards personal salvation in fear and trembling, were the question to have been decided, once and for all, by the preordination of God. The idea of predestination is as heretical to the natural, rational mind as is the doctrine of free will to the orthodox Muslim. But this type of criticism makes the mistake of regarding religion only as a system of thought, the separate components of which must not, and cannot, stand in opposition to one another. But religion, as we know, is completely different. It is quite able to embrace a *complexio oppositorum*, a union of opposites. A paradox, such as the doctrine of predestination, may well be the only possible way of expressing the truth that our salvation rests entirely in the hand of God. The paradox would be destructive, were one really to draw all its consequences and apply it, for example, also to the question of man's unconditional responsibility. But the believer does not draw these consequences. That which has to follow, in the opinion of the critics, does not happen at all. The assertion has often been made that the petrification of Islamic culture into a state of conservatism and dormant passivity has come about as a result of fatalism, that is, of the doctrine of absolute predestination. I shall leave aside the question whether this is a correct view where Islam is concerned. But Calvin, too, taught predestination, and there have never existed more active and expansionist cultures than those of the Anglo-Saxon peoples. Thus while in theory man *must* submit to indifference and stultifying weakness, what actually happens is the opposite. Dhū'n-Nūn describes how the believer feels, when he knows himself to be included in the divine plan of predestination: "I am grace of Thy grace, predestination from Thy predestination. I run in Thy grace, I wander freely in Thy predestination. I increase in growth according to Thy prescience and do not diminish according to Thy firm decree. From that position in which Thou hast placed me, no one shall be able to cast me out, save Thou alone. I am unable of myself to flee from sin, except Thy love awaken me."[3] Dhū'n-Nūn, we may observe, does not find the thought of predestination paralyzing, but liberating. It prompts action and inspires confidence. Man is never able to feel more free than when God is his Lord, completely.

Further, it might seem that one is *forced* to the conclusion that if God is all in all, even my sins must be His doing, and I myself must be left without any responsibility. But the believer does not bow to this argument in any way. He can say, without hesitation: "My sin, O God, belongs to my self, its innermost essence is my own self. My love belongs to Thee, its innermost essence is Thy self." And then we find this climactic contradiction: "Love, which is Thy gift, I devote to Thee by my free will. Sin, which is of my own self, I commit against my will."[4]

For the Sufis the thought of predestination becomes a certainty of God's prevenient grace. It is God who takes the initiative. It is not through myself, but through God that I come to know Him; it is through God Himself that I am able to obey Him. Common legalistic piety says that God's love is earned by obeying and loving Him. God's love for us is bestowed as a reward for our good behavior. Aḥmad ibn Abī'l-Ḥawārī makes another slight concession to this idea: "A sign of the love of God is that one loves to obey God. When God loves His servant, the servant loves Him. And the servant is not able to love God, except God Himself begin by loving him. And this He does when He sees the servant strive to gain His good pleasure."[5] In itself the effort to please God, even though it is insufficient *per se*, awakens God's saving love.

Muḥāsibī, on the other hand, turns the doctrine of legalistic piety completely upside down: "That which comes first in the love of God is obedience to Him, and that obedience proceeds from God Himself and has its source in Him. It is He who teaches His chosen ones to know Him, guiding them to obey Him; He enters into a loving covenant with them, although it is not He who needs them, but they who need Him. Thereupon he places love for Himself as a token in their hearts, and Himself envelops them in the light which radiates from their words by the power of their love. When He has done this, He brings them in His joy before His angels, that the angels, whom He has deemed worthy to inhabit His heavens, may love them. Before He has created His beloved ones, He praises them, and before they have praised Him, He thanks them. For He knows in His prescience, that He will one day lift them to that high spiritual level which He has destined and predetermined for them."[6] Everything—obedience, the love of God and those marvellous, inspired words that bear witness to the wonderful experience of divine love—these things are a gift and an act of God, and of His free grace.

Love, then, is not a matter of our having loved God: "At the beginning," Abū Yazīd says, "I imagined that it was I who thought of God, knew Him and loved Him. When I reached the end, I realized that He had thought of me before I thought of Him; that He had known me before I knew Him; that His love for me preceded my love for Him; and that He had sought me first, so that I could then seek Him."[7] In another Sufi saying, attributed to the prophet Moses, this same idea is expressed in a manner reminiscent of Pascal's famous aphorism: You would not seek me, had you not already found me. The soul asks: "Tell me, where art Thou, Lord, so that I can seek to come to Thee?" And God answers: "When you begin to seek to come to Me, you have already come to Me."[8] To be a *murīd*, a seeker after God, is an honorific title for the beginner on the path of devotion. A higher degree is that of being one who is sought (*murād*). "He who seeks God is led by the power of knowledge; he who is sought, led by God's own power. He who seeks is walking, but he who is sought is flying."[9] The conviction that the true love is God's love for us, and not ours for Him, gives strength and liberation. When a pious man was told: "You are a man who loves God," he answered: "No, not a man who loves, but one who is loved. He who loves is still under coercion."[10] In Christian parlance, we would say: he is still in bondage to the Law.

There is no other religion for which Schleiermacher's well-known aphorism: "Religion is the feeling of absolute dependence," is more apt than that of Islam. "There is no God, and no one is able to do what He does. No one can do harm or do good, give or keep back, make ill or make well, elevate or debase, create and sustain, ill and bring to life, hold at rest or set in motion, save He alone."[11] God is in fact the only active power in existence. Muslim theologians have often used the puppet play as an image of human beings, who think that they act independently, when it actually is God who pulls the strings.[12]

The positive side of the feeling of dependence is a boundless confidence and trust in the God who is all in all. According to Islam, complete trust in God is the sum of all devotion, an ideal perpetually to be striven after, but never wholly attainable. Dārānī said: "There is not one of the spiritual stages of the pious that I do not know and firmly possess, except that of blessed trust in God. Of that, I only feel a faint breeze, which does not last."[13]

The term which I have here translated by 'trust in God' is however a typical example of the fact that terms and expressions which encompass, as it were in a condensed form, a complete religious way of thinking or style of life, are essentially untranslateable. For the seaker of Arabic, the word used here, *tawakkul*, evokes a particular, characteristic image. The word means "to trust someone in the same way as I would trust my *wakīl*," that is to say the person whom I have chosen to be my procurator, my *homme d'affaires*, to look after my business and to govern and dispose on my behalf. To trust in God means that man leaves all care in the hand of God and allows Him both to will and to act for him. "All happiness consists of allowing God to govern for us according to His good pleasure. And every unhappiness and all misery is based on our desire to arrange things for ourselves."[14] This complete handing over of all action to God may assume a purely quietist character: "The first step in trusting God is for the servant to place himself in God's hands like a dead man in the hands of the person laying him out. He turns the corpse as he wishes, and it neither moves nor shows any will of its own."[15]

The Sufis love aphoristic turns of phrases, and such a statement does not necessarily prove that they actually passively and willy-nilly left it to God to make every decision for them. Nor was Cardinal Newman a quietist because he wrote, in his wonderful hymn "Lead, kindly light":

> I love to choose and see my path, but now
> Lead Thou me on.

But we do not dispute the fact that within Sufism, some questionable conclusions were drawn from the doctrine of trust in God. Dāwūd at-Ṭāʾī was such a pious man that he regarded it as unnecessary, and inconsistent with real trust in God, to sweep the spiders' webs off his ceiling, to close a window to shut out the sun's heat, or to mend a fur-lined mantle when the hairs started showing through the torn fabric.[16]

Many ascetics have interpreted the dictum that "God will provide for us" in a highly literal sense. When Ibn Adham asked a monk: "What do you live on?" the holy man replied: "Ask my Lord, where He fetches food for me."[17] Sufi legends are full of fantastic narrative about saints who travel through the desert wilderness without carrying food or water. When the time comes for a meal, the holy man simply stamps on the ground, and immediately finds a table laden with delicious dishes, and with cool, scented water in silver bowls, ready for him to wash in. However, it was an actual practice among the Sufis for pious wanderers to set out on their journeys without carrying food. "That was the custom of the friends of God," it is said, "so that if the wanderer should die, on his journey, trusting in God, it would be the duty of the one who killed him, namely God, to take responsibility and make restitution."[18] It was said of a well-known Sufi, Ibrāhīm al-Khawwāṣ, that he used to travel 'trusting in God', that is to say, without food for his journey. There were, however, four things that he always wanted to keep by him, both on his travels and at home: a waterskin, a rope, a needle and a thread, and a pair of scissors, for "these things do not belong to the things of the world."[19] But he made one well-considered exception: there were, he maintained, three cases in which consideration for others demanded that one should carry food on a journey: when sitting with one's brothers in the mosque; when on a sea-voyage; and when travelling with a caravan.[20] To save food from one day to the next is not however consistent with a genuine trust in God. Nor should one worry in any way about tomorrow's food: "God does not require of you to do tomorrow's work today. Therefore you should not be so unreasonable as to request tomorrow's sustenance from Him today."[21]

From the stories of the *Thousand and One Nights* we recall that when the hero falls into mortal danger, he often acts in a manner totally different from what we would expect of a hero: "The light before his face became darkness, his teeth chattered and his knees trembled." In his fear he then pronounces that protective formula which is the final refuge of an individual in peril: "There is no power and no strength save in God. Behold, we belong to God and we shall return to Him." This sounds pious enough, but the Sufis agree that this is no way for the true believer to speak, since it contradicts his trust in God.[22] Junayd explains: "That is how a frightened man speaks, and if one is frightened it proves that one does not, in fact trust God."

If one believes sincerely that God reigns over all things and governs all things, and that future is in His hands, one should not speak about the future as though it depended upon ourselves in the least. We know that the Apostle James emphasizes this in his Letter, and the Sufis express it in the same way. "It is characteristic of the friends of God," says Sahl, "that they always make reservations in what they say. He who says: 'I shall do such-and-such' without adding 'God willing', will be held responsible for it on the Day of Judgment."[23] Among Christians it is only individual and particularly scrupulous believers who add a D.V. (*Deus volens*) to each expression put in the future tense. The Muslim, however, constantly adds an *inshāllāh*, as soon as he mentions anything which is still in the future; far too often this becomes merely a comfortable excuse for laziness and indolence.

One question that has frequently occupied the minds of pious believers is whether or not it is right to go to a doctor when one is ill. Is it not inconsistent with real trust in God, to be unwilling to accept what God sends us and instead seek help from another human being against God? As a rule the Sufis, too, declined medical help. Dhū'n-Nūn once wrote to a sick friend: "Illness is a gift. One should make it a bosom friend, and let pain and anxiety serve as a reminder of where to find true healing."[24] Sahl had an illness of a kind that is usually curable. But he refused to go to a doctor. People asked him why, and he replied: "When the Beloved strikes you, you feel no pain."[25] Otherwise, he considered medicines to be "God's merciful gift to those who are weak in faith." Nevertheless it is preferable not to use them, since "the one who takes medicine, even if it were only a glass of cold water, will be asked on the Day of Judgment, why he took it."[26] Pentecostals and other more recent Christian healing sects, as we know, similarly consider it a sign of lack of faith to consult doctors. The true believer should resort to prayer and the laying on of hands in faith. The Sufis are still more pious. The very fact of praying to God for health is a sign of spiritual weakness, implying discontent with God's providence and a lack of trust in His gracious will, should one ask Him to change that which He has ordained. On one occasion Junayd was ill with a fever. A disciple came to him and asked: "O Master", he cried, "Tell God in order that He may restore thee to health." Junayd said: "Last night I was about to tell Him, but a voice whispered in my heart; 'Thy body belongs to Me; I keep it well or ill, as I please. Who art thou, that thou shouldst interfere with My property?'"[27] One might well ask what the doctor really is able to do, since it is God who bestows health or illness, without any active involvement on our part. According to a Sufi story, Moses asked God: "Lord, from whom comes illness and its healing?" "From Myself."

"And what, then, does the doctor do?"

Whereupon the Lord replies, with gentle irony: "He collects his fee and keeps My servants in good spirits, until I Myself come to them, either to grant them health or to decide the matter otherwise."[28]

Now, if God has undertaken to support the believer, should man then take over His responsibility by working for his own livelihood? There were in fact Sufis who believed that unlimited trust in God demanded that the individual should live like the lilies of the field. Bishr had supported himself for a period by spinning thread, just as Gandhi did. Then one of the his pious friends wrote to him: "I hear that you have a spindle to help you make a living. But if God should take away your vision and your hearing from you now, who would then support you?" Those words impressed themselves on Bishr's mind so strongly that he let the spindle fall from his hand and stopped working.[29] Sarī had once been a merchant, but gave up working for a living and lived for a time off his sister's earnings as a spinner. Later he decided that even this means of support was less than pious and declared: "Since my refusal to go on living off my sister's earnings, God has charged the world to give me support and serve me."[30] After that he lived on the gifts of the faithful, which he considered acceptable if one were able by this means to feel entirely dependent upon God alone. For God does not want His servant to find his livelihood where he expects it. Where he himself looks for it, God does not permit him to find it. Later God provides it from some entirely unexpected source.[31] However, one should take great care not to make oneself dependent upon people's generosity and goodness. One should receive gifts exclusively from the hand of God. "You should never thank a man for that which God gives, nor should you blame a man for that which He does not want to give us."[32]

A Sufi is not allowed to beg and should, preferably, appear proudly reluctant when offered a gift. Wealthy people ought to feel it a great privilege should the holy man deign to accept a gift from their hands. A man came to Junayd, wanting to give him five hundred gold coins for distribution among his disciples. Junayd asked him: "Do you want your wealth to increase?"

"Yes."

"Then keep your money. You need it more than we do."[33]

On another occasion a man came all the way from Khorasan, to give him a sum of money on condition that he would not distribute the money among the poor, but use it for his own personal needs. But Junayd raised objections: "How long would I have to live to be able to spend all this gold?"

The man from Khorasan said: "I do not want you to spend the money on vegetables and vinegar, but on sweets and delicacies."

Then Junayd was touched, and accepted the money. And the man from Khorasan said: "No one in Baghdad has shown me as great a favor as you have done."[34]

In practice the classical Sufis had however completely abandoned the spiritual ideals of holy indolence and mendicacy. If they received gifts, they gave good value for them by their teaching; in any case there was hardly any other known method of paying a teacher of science or spirituality in the society of their day. Most Sufis considered it not only permissible to work for their living, but regarded it as a duty for those who needed to do so, and in all circumstances as being praiseworthy. Bishr once said to a man who had become so devout that he no longer worked: "I have heard that you do not go to the bazaar any more. You ought to do so. It is your duty to work honestly for a living and to be frugal in all your expenditure. I would prefer you all to spend the night hungry but with money in your purses, than to go to sleep filled but with your purses empty."[35] Dārānī, too, maintained that one ought not to renounce the world in such a way as to become a burden on others.[36] "It is not piety, that you set your feet in the ranks of those at prayer, while someone else is crumbling your bread for you. And nothing good lives in the heart of one who sits piously at home without working, but all the time waiting for someone to come knocking on the door and enter with a gift."[37] Junayd even thought that the devotee should go to the bazaar, albeit as a gesture, in order not to seem to despise honest work, or to give the appearance of being more pious than other men. In Junayd's hall of instruction, one day the talk was of those people who sit in the mosque trying to imitate the Sufis, without in fact fulfilling the conditions for membership of their community. Such people used to speak ill of those who traded in the bazaar. Then Junayd said: "Many a man in the bazaars would have the right to enter the mosque, take any one of those hypocrites by the ear, lead him outside and take his place. I know a man who goes to work every day in the bazaar, and his daily acts of devotion are three hundred prostrations and thirty thousand doxologies." The listeners understood that he was alluding to himself.[38] He would come to the bazaar every day and open his stall. Then he closed the curtains, made three hundred prostrations and then returned home.[39]

"Those who go to the bazaars" are merchants and tradesmen. Business or trades thus are worthy occupations for pious man. Sufism belongs completely within the context of city life, and agriculture can hardly be considered as a suitable profession for a mystic. Public office of any kind is an impossibility, since that would make man dependent upon godless officials. If one looks at the history of mysticism as a whole, one might perhaps regard shoemaking as an especially pious occupation. Remarkably enough, the mystics of Islam considered the most suitable work for a holy man to be that of clothier. It is said: "If the blessed in heaven could engage in business they would deal in fabrics, and if the damned in hell were able to follow a profession, it would be that of money-lending." Four types of work are less highly regarded: weaver, cotton-spinner, laundryman and teacher. In the first three, it is argued, one works largely with women, and that is morally dangerous; and in the fourth case one works with unintelligent children, which weakens a man's mind."[40]

God governs and disposes. The believer should therefore face the matters and events of the future with confident trust. Concerning the past he should show himself content with the will of God, rest in the will of God. When I translate the Sufi term *riḍā* by 'resting in the will of God', I must point out that here we are not dealing with a submissive resignation, unprotestingly accepting that which God has decreed once and for all. "To rest in the will of God is to turn towards that which God has sent, with strength and joy, for the devout man is sure that his Lord always does what is best for him, Who is most merciful and Who best knows what is of benefit to him. Resting in the will of God is therefore in itself will and approbation: to desire that which God does and to be content with Him in one's heart."[41]

Illness and adversity should be welcomed by the true believer. They signify "that God is thinking graciously of His servant."[42] For "God shows incessant concern for His servants by way of tribulations, just as a father demonstrates constant care for his own family through acts of kindness."[43] Everything, even the greatest difficulties, should be gratefully received from the hand of God. The mystic must realize that there is much in the acts of God that must appear to us incomprehensible, offensive, and disturbing. Many a time it would appear as though He desires not our success but our destruction, as though He were intentionally leading us into overpowering temptations and even wants to seduce us into disobedience and sin. This manner of acting the Sufis call God's 'ruse' (*makr*). "God has hidden His ruse in His mildness, His betrayal in His goodness and His condemnation in His bestowal of honour."[44] The true believer can only submit, in humble obedience, to the inscrutable will of God: "If He meets me with a ruse in His omnipotence, I shall meet Him with humility in my dependence upon Him."[45] And there remains the ultimate possibility of seeking help from God against God. "Dhū'n-Nūn was asked about those misfortunes by which the disciple is so deceived that he loses touch with God. He answered: 'That happens through God's acts of grace, His miracles and signs (which He allows to be performed through the disciple's hands).'

'But before the disciple has attained such a high spiritual level?'

'Then it is accomplished when he changes the prescribed times of prayer on his own authority, when people show him honour, when he enjoys the (spiritual) gatherings and when he has numerous numerous followers. God preserves us from His ruse and deceit.'"

"I have," said Dārānī, "only perceived the passing fragrance of resting in the will of God. And yet I know that if God were to take all people to Paradise, and consign myself alone to hell, I would rest content with His will."[46] It is well known that many mystics have gone so far that they have been able to feel a certain perverse pleasure in pain itself. Abū Yazīd could even claim to long for God's punishment:

> Thee I desire; yet not that Thou reward me,
> I desire Thee that I Thy punishment may suffer;
> Since all the I request Thou has already granted,
> Except my relishing that pain which is Thy punishment.[44]

"I have no other head than Christ and no other creed than love," declared the English mystic Richard Rolle, an older contemporary of Wycliffe. If the word 'Christ' were altered to 'God', the Sufi mystics could happily make this statement their own. If a Sufi were to express in one word the significance of his relationship to God, he would certainly use the word 'love'. A religion which is as severe and as rigid in its attitude as is Islam, has not found it easy to use the word 'love' to describe man's relationship to God. As Louis Massignon has demonstrated,[48] both theologians and traditionists during the first Muslim centuries curtly dismissed the gentle voice of the mysticism of love. It should however be emphasized that the word was nonetheless often used in circles of devotees, as early as the second and third generation of Muslims. Ḥasan al-Baṣrī even used a terminology so advanced as to talk about the intoxication of love: "The lover is drunk and he does not wake up from his drunkenness until he sees the beloved."[49] An older contemporary also spoke of the cup of love: "My God, Thou givest me, without my asking Thee. How couldst Thou then refuse me, when I ask? O God, I beseech Thee that Thou allow Thy greatness to dwell in my heart and that Thou permit me to drink from the cup of Thy love."[50] But it was only among the Sufis that love was to become the great keyword of man's relationship to God. In mysticism love is both the path and the goal. Like Catherine of Genoa, the Sufi often calls his God, simply, the Beloved. And just as Suso addressed the soul's Beloved in the language of the German *Minnesang*, the Sufi mystics also used the traditional vocabulary and phraseology of secular love-poetry. However, the language of Sufi mysticism remains within the sphere of falling in love and infatuation, and never speaks of actual conjugal love.[51] The words 'bridegroom' and 'bride' are never used.

He who loves God does not desire, does not think about or seek anything other than Him. "Why do you never travel?" someone once asked Abū Yazīd. He answered: "My Beloved does not go away, and I remain with Him."[52] God, and He alone, and nothing else in the world! He who truly loves God does not seek His gifts but only Himself. "Ordinary people," Junayd says, "love God for the sake of His blessings. Therefore their love grows and diminishes according to God's dealings with them. The chosen ones love God for what He is and for all His perfect qualities. They can never cease to love Him, even should He withdraw all His blessings from them."[53] In Junayd's words:

> My God, my God, should'st Thou yet show me
> Cold aspect, and turn Thy face away from me,
> Never from longing for Thee could my soul escape,
> Though I were even to leave this life behind.[54]

The heavenly Friend also watches jealously, lest anything else usurp His place in the human heart. There is a Sufi legend about an Israelite ascetic, who had served God for four hundred years on a desert island. His hair had grown so long that it caught in the branches of the trees when he walked among them. One day as he was walking through the forest he discovered a bird's nest in a tree. Then he moved his place of prayer close to the tree in order to observe the bird and its young. Soon, however, he heard a voice, saying: "You have grown close to someone other than Myself. Therefore I shall move you down two steps below your former spiritual level."[55] He who has truly come to know the love of God cannot understand how one could possibly abandon Him.[56]

Dhū'n-Nūn was also of the opinion that the one who turns away from God has never reached Him; he has only gone part of the way to Him.[57]

Like the spiritual states and degrees, love too was discussed and analysed *ad infinitum*. Generally, three stages were distinguished: love, friendship and passion. Thus the highest level of love is passion. In Arabic poetry love has a more intense colour and rapid pulse than in the Northern setting. It is like glowing coals and consuming flame, compared to a pale and anaemic *Schwärmerei*. It is not enough for the lover to walk alone, yearning and dreaming. He grows thin, sallow, and transparent, is consumed by fever, laid on his sick-bed and, if worst comes to worst and his beloved remains unmoved, he will die of longing. When he meets the adored one, he falls senseless at her feet, and may even faint, never to awaken again. Al-Ghazālī provides in his work *Iḥyā' 'ulūm al-dīn* (*The Revivification of the Knowledge of the Faith*),[58] numerous anecdotes describing the true nature of love. "On one occasion," says 'Umar ibn al-Ḥārith, "I was visiting a friend, and with us there was also a young man, who was passionately enamoured of a singer, who was also part of the gathering. She plucked the strings of her lute and sang:

The tears of the lover show
That all his pride he has surrendered,
Since there is none in the world
To whom he dares confess his pain.

When she had finished, the young man said: "What beautiful words, O ruler of my heart! Will you allow me to die?" The cruel young woman replied: "Of course, die at once!" Then he laid his head on a pillow, closed his lips and his eyes; we touched him and behold! then we discovered that he was dead." In the same way, the one thought in the mind of the true believer should also be that of obeying the Beloved to the very end:

Were my loved one to say: die in willing obedience,
At once I would say to death's herald: I welcome you in![59]

In this manner Sufi poets describe passion, the perfected love of God. It has struck the believer like a consuming sickness, burning in his heart like a fever and breaking down his physical frame. The mystics, too, belong with "jene Asra, welche sterben, wenn sie lieben".[60] Dhū'n-Nūn gives poetic expression to this feeling:

I shall die, but never can die the heat of my love for Thee.
Daily and hourly my work I neglect for the sake of my love.
Thee I desire, the only desire of my heart is for Thee.

> Thou with Thy riches alone canst meet this poor one's need.
> Thou art my highest desire, the goal of all my longing,
> The place where my troubles I tell, the hidden world of my soul.
> Thou hast given my heart a secret to keep, that may not be told,
> Though my sickness be long, though long may be my time of
> distress.
> Within my heart I conceal that which is known to Thee only.
> Not for my husband, nor yet for my friend may it be revealed.
> Thou hast made my heart sick with a sickness that penetrates
> all things,
> My strength it has broken, no power remains save my secret.[61]

Sarī was often heard to recite the following verse, probably often sung by dark-eyed women singers at love-feasts in the city of the Caliphs:

> No longer the day brings me joy, no longer the night brings balm.
> What matters it whether the night be long or short its measure?
> Love-sick I watch its passing hours in perpetual pain.
> By day I am constantly torn by sorrow and tortured thoughts.[62]

As with Catherine of Genoa, for the Sufi mystic, too, love may literally bring about his death. Junayd relates how he was sitting with his teacher Sarī, during the latter's final illness. "He was dressed only in a thin mantle and I saw his body like the body of someone seriously ill and utterly emaciated. His face was blotchy, yellow and bloodshot, and he said: 'Look at my body! If I were to tell you that what I suffer is caused by love, then I would be telling the truth.'"[63] That true love means that the heart suffers and bleeds to death, is shown in a delicate anecdote about Dhū'n-Nūn. One day, when he was speaking in a particularly moving way about love, a bird came and perched on the ground in front of him. It struck its beak against the ground again and again, until it began to bleed and then it died.[64]

Pleasure and pain are indissolubly united in the mystical experience. The road to union with God runs through struggle, despair, and darkness of the soul. Saint Theresa speaks of "the dark night of the soul," through which the chosen have to fight their way. Junayd describes the way to the union with God as a journey through the wilderness, filled with all the horror and danger associated with wandering through the trackless Arabian desert. The road leads through "deserts when you perish and wildernesses where you are destroyed, where you cannot wander without a guide and which you cannot pass through without being parted, for ever, from your home." It begins when the soul is suddenly "taken deep into a space without limit. . . . There you find yourself in a place, whose safety is fear, whose intimacy is isolation, whose light is darkness, whose comfort is adversity, whose presence is absence, whose life is death. In that place the seeker finds no goal, the wanderer finds no food along the way, the fugitive finds no refuge. To encounter this place is to be uprooted, the first of its remarkable events is that a judgment is pronounced, the reward of wandering through it is fear. And if its deep waves pass over you, you will be broken by their force, you will disappear in the water, you will be submerged in its murky depths, where you will remain lost. Who will help you out of that which has happened to you? Who can lead you out of this peril? . . . Take care, and care again: Take care! Many a man who has approached this task has been caught; many a man who has shouldered the burden has broken down, perishing by his own neglect and hastening to his death. May God grant you and me a place among those who will be saved."[65]

Pain and suffering follow, even after the bliss of union itself; the light of transfiguration is dimmed, the heavenly Friend is gone and the wonderful sense of His presence is succeeded by the bitter pangs of loss. "While I was travelling," Dhū'n-Nūn says, "one dark night among the hills near Jerusalem, I head a sad voice and loud weeping. The voice said: 'O, what loneliness after such intimacy, what alienation after such security of home, what poverty after such riches, what humiliation after such glory!' I followed after the one who cried this, until I came close to him, myself still inundated with tears over his weeping. When morning dawned, so that I could see him, I found him to be an old man, thin and dry like an old leather bag. And I said to him: 'God be merciful to you, how you lament!' He replied: 'Let me be. I had a heart, and I have lost it.' And he sang:

> Once I had a heart, together we lived in dalliance.
> But love smote it, and my heart was consumed in the flames.[66]

It is bitter to experience the parting as an intolerable fate, brought about by those changes of feeling which the believer himself is able neither to understand nor to control. The unseen Friend departs, because such is the course of life, meeting, and parting. But the parting is so much more bitter, when one knows that it is caused by one's own ingratitude, neglect and sloth. Dhū'n-Nūn once heard one of the friends of God sing while he held on to the curtain of the Ka'ba:

> I have tasted the bliss of union. Thou has also granted me
> A longing for Thee that pierces all sorrow and pain.

Then he said to himself: "He has shown Himself to be tolerant towards you, and you have not turned away. He has lowered His veil upon you, and you have not been ashamed. He has removed from you the bliss of His fellowship, and you have not perished. O Thou Glorious One, what has come upon me? When I stand before Thee, I am overcome by drowsiness, and that prevents me from feeling the blissful solace I find in Thee." After that he sang again:

> Thy threat of parting has made my heart fearful. Nothing I know
> So bitter to taste as the pain of parting, so full of distress.
> Enough if I say that it will divide us, and bring back afresh
> That sorrow I once bade farewell with joy and relief.[67]

However, this spiritual love poetry is not exclusively in the elegiac mood. Love is also an unbounded joy, an intoxication. That Dionysian symbolism, which would at a later date give Sufism an undeservedly bad reputation, already meets us here in the Sufi classics. Love is "a cup of burning fire, when it invades our senses and makes its home in our souls."[68]

> By the heat of our union my heart has been wounded.
> My longing increases, my love all can see.
> A drink Thou hast offered, my heart to revive,
> From the chalice of passion, drawn from the ocean of love.

Thus sings Abū Yazīd.[69] Beduin poetry often describes how the young man secretly visits his beloved among her kinsfolk, the risks to which the lovers expose themselves, and the wild happiness of their covert meetings. Mystical poetry uses identical imagery. Junayd once heard about a girl who circumambulated the Ka'ba, singing of her heavenly Friend meanwhile:

> My Friend will not remain secret. Though oft I have hidden Him,
> To me He came. He set up His tent and abode by my side.
> Thinking of Him, my heart beats aloud with the heat of my
> longing.
> Though I depart from beside my Beloved, He comes to me.
> He comes—and makes me as nothing. New life He bestows on me
> From Him and for Him. His bliss He imparts for my joy and
> delight.[70]

The level of friendship is of a different hue. It is that kind of friendship which God showed to Abraham, he who was called *Khalīl Allāh*, the friend of God. "In this degree," Junayd says, "God's servant knows that God loves him. He is therefore able to say: 'by that right, that distinction and position of honour I have with Thee, by Thy love for me!' Those who have attained this level live in full intimacy with God and are His close friends. All anxious respect and fear of God has been brought to an end. They are able to say things that might appear to others as unbelief, because they know that God loves them."[71] Sven Lidman in one of his books told of a Negro who was said to be particularly successful in his prayers. When he prayed, he did not speak as a nervous supplicant, but he delivered, in an insistent, almost threatening voice, his unconditional demand that God should hear his prayer.[72] Al-Ghazālī tells a similar story. "Once upon a time it happened that God had not allowed rain to fall on the land of Israel for a period of seven years. All prayers for rain were in vain. Finally God said to Moses: 'I cannot hear your prayers, because your hearts are darkened by sin, so that you pray without firmness of faith. Send for my servant Baruch.' Eventually they discovered Baruch who was found to be a poor Negro slave, and he undertook to pray." He began his prayer by giving the Lord a veritable telling-off: "Is this the way You usually act? Is this in accordance with Your mercy? What is wrong with You? Have Your eyes grown weak, or have the winds ceased to obey Your command, or have Your supplies run out? Or are You perhaps angered by our transgressions? Are You then not the God who forgave, long before You had created us sinners?' Moses was frightened by such boldness, but God said: 'Such is my servant Baruch. He makes me laugh, three times every day.' And rain fell in streams, so that the people waded knee-deep in water."[73] It was said of pious Sufis that they too spoke to God with the same bold intimacy.

Undeniably there are many aspects of the Sufis' love of God which appear strange to us. But there are also simple and moving expressions of deep and genuine feeling. "It is nothing strange that I love Thee, I who am a poor slave. What is strange is that Thou lovest me, Thou who are a mighty King."[74] When [Abū Yazīd] was happy and overwhelmed by his feelings, he used to exclaim: "To Thee belong majesty, beauty and perfection. Thou art that Thou art: for ever and ever! Thy love for me is pre-eternal."[75]

"Give up bread for ever, and yet thou wilt always desire it. More than bread, God is worthy of thy longing for Him."[76]

There are also testimonies to a love that has become the moral power that completely grasps and totally changes a person. Perfect love, union with God, means that the self is killed and eradicated. Love of God is the annihilation of all expressions of will, all personal characteristics, all needs. Ḥallāj and Abū Yazīd were not the first to speak of a union, in which human and divine become one. Previously Sarī had said: "The love between two is not perfect, until the one says, when speaking of the other: 'I'."[77] On this issue, the language of Sufism can be misunderstood. It has been interpreted as a change of being in which the human self disappears completely, is eradicated and annihilated in the divine sea of light. Man is no longer man, but God. In Indian mysticism, especially theistic mysticism, the final union with the divine is frequently of this kind. The pious Vaishnava (worshipper of Vishnu) sings: "I *am* Vishnu, and all is mine. I am all, and all is in me. I am eternal and without end, and as the place where the highest Self resides, I am called Brahman." Vishnu is in all and all is in him, "like the bracelet, the crown and the ring are all of one and the same gold, as water vapour enters the earth and becomes one with it, once the wind which brought it forth has calmed." Union with God thus has a highly concrete, almost material character.

Sufi mysticism, too, uses very strong words concerning the total eradication of the human personality. "Know this: that when the knowledge of God is great within you and your heart is filled with it and your breast is open by your having dedicated yourself entirely to Him; and that when your being is purified to make supplication unto Him, and your mind united with God; then your characteristics, your own attributes are obliterated and your knowledge is illuminated by God Himself," says Junayd.[78] He is also said to have stated: "I have read many books, but I have never found anything so instructive as this verse:

> When I say: "What is my sin?' she says in reply.
> 'Thy existence is a sin with which no other sin can be compared.'[79]

Thus it seems as though existence as a separate personality itself were the root of all sin. Fundamentally, however , this is not what is meant. We are not dealing with a metaphysical change, but a change that is religious and moral. Union with God signifies that God's will becomes man's will, totally, and that man is changed, in a moral sense, into the image of God. We might say that he assumes God's attributes. "Love," says Junayd, "means that the qualities of the beloved replace your own."[80] Dārānī informs us as to which of God's attributes it is that He bestows upon His friends: they are "generosity, gentleness, knowledge, wisdom, goodness, mercy, forbearance".[81] To be close to someone who possesses the knowledge of God is therefore like being close to God himself, since "he is an image of God's perfect attributes."[82]

One who corresponds to the ideal thus described has attained union with God. This is the real meaning of the "disappearance," *fanā*,' a concept that has been compared, somewhat rashly, to the Buddhist concept of *nirvāna*. Al-Kharrāz was asked: "What characterizes the one who has attained the disappearance?' He replied: 'The disappearance of all joy and happiness in this world and the next, except that of rejoicing in God."[83] To the Sufi, the disappearance of the self has a meaning no different, in principle, than it has to the Apostle Paul, when he says:

" . . . it is no longer I who live, but Christ who lives in me" (Gal. 2:20, RSV). Sufi mysticism uses the term *baqā'*, 'abiding'. "'Disappearance' is to disappear in God through God. 'Abiding' is to live with God."[84]

I have come to the end of my presentation. I have tried to describe Sufism, not as a system of thought but as living religion, and to convey an idea of its spirit and its soul. That is why I have allowed it to speak largely in its own words. But perhaps the journey has not been in vain. We have seen how Muslim asceticism went through a remarkable development. This took place without direct influence from Christianity, but not perhaps without being influenced by latent Christian ideas, which lived on—in an extraordinary way, like rays separated from their source of light—as a part of Islam's own tradition. Thus asceticism came to be reshaped into a mystical piety, which in its spirit and essence comes closer to the Gospel than any other non-Christian religion known to us.

The study of this devotional piety ought to give occasion for reflection among those Christian theologians who draw the boundaries of divine revelations so narrowly that it illuminates only one point, leaving everything else belonging to the world of religion in absolute darkness. Perhaps therefore even this remote province in the wide world of faith might in the end cast fresh light on the word of the Old Testament prophet: "For from the rising of the sun to its setting my name is great among the nations, and in every place incense is offered to my name, and a pure offering; for my name is great among the nations, says the Lord of hosts" (Malachi 1:11, RSV).

NOTES

Tor Andrae

1. The only complete biography of Andrae is in Swedish: Geo Widengren, *Tor Andrae* (Stockholm 1949). Twenty separate memorial essays are contained in Ove Hassler and Robert Murray (eds.), *Tor Andrae in memoriam* (Stockholm n.d.). Here I should like to record my gratitude to Professor Carl-Martin Edsman of Uppsala for making available photocopies of other book reviews and memorial tributes to Andrae.

2. This work was actually produced without capitals for the German nouns, an eccentricity of the editor of the series in which it appeared.

3. Geo Widengren, in *T.A. in memoriam*, p. 108.

4. H.S. Nyberg, in ibid., p. 67.

5. Ibid., p. 76.

6. Tor Andrae, 'Mystik och social gemenskap,' in *Till Arkebiskop Söderbloms sextioårsdag* (Stockhold, 1926), p. 26.

7. Ibid., p. 25.

8. Tor Andrae, *Georg Wallin: resor, forskningar och öden* (Stockholm, 1936 - first published by the Swedish Academy in 1934), p. 5 f.

9. Letter to Einar Odhner, November 26, 1924, quoted in *T.A. in memoriam*, p. 33 f.

10. Tor Andrae, *Muhammed, hans liv och hans tro* (Stockholm, 1930), p. 6.

11. Edvard Rodhe, in *T.A. in memoriam*, p. 49.

Introduction

1. [Louis Massignon's studies of al-Ḥallāj began in 1913 with his edition of Ḥallāj's *Kitāb aṭ-ṭawāsīn*; his opus magnum, *La Passion d'al-Ḥosayn ibn Manṣūr*

al-Ḥallāj, appeared in 1922 in two volumes and was reissued in four volumes in 1975; this edition was published in the English translation of Herbert Mason, in the Bollingen Series, Princeton University Press, 1982. Besides, Massignon has devoted numerous other works to the elucidation of al-Ḥallāj's thought, such as the *Quatre textes hallajiennes*, Paris 1922; *Essai sur les origines du lexique technique de la mystique musulmane*, 1922; "Le divân d'al-Ḥallâj, Essai de reconstitution, in *Journal Asiatique*, 1931, and, together with Paul Kraus, the *Abhār al-Ḥallāj*, (Paris, 1936), 3rd. ed. 1957. In numerous articles he has tried to show the survival of Ḥallāj in Islamic literature and thought.]

2. Translator's note: Esaias Tegnér (1782–1846) Swedish bishop, was a writer and poet of the Romantic period, while remaining critical of some aspects of German Romantic philosophy.

3. as-Sulamī, *Ṭabaqāt aṣ-ṣūfīya*, Ms. Berlin Cod. WE 139, fol. 12a [= ed. Nūraddīn Sharība, Cairo 1954, 87].

4. al- cArūsī, *Natā'ij al-afkār* (Bulaq 129oH/1873), 4 vols.; 1: 141.

5. Hujwīrī, *Kashf al- maḥjūb*, transl. by Reynold A. Nicholson, (London-Leiden, 1911), 189. Hereafter Hujwīrī, *Kashf*.

6. al-Yāficī, *Rauḍ ar-riyāḥīn*, at the margin of ath-Thaclabī, *cArā'is al-majālis*, Cairo, 13o3 H/ 1885–6, 32 f.

Chapter I

1. Tor Andrae, in: *Bibelforskåren*, Year 38, 107: Cf. for the problem also C.A. Tritton, *The Caliphs and their non-Muslim subjects*, (London, 1930). *GW*. [See also the first chapter of Marijan Molé, *Les Mystiques Musulmans*, (Paris, 1965), which in many cases supports Andrae's theses without having access to his Swedish work].

2. Massignon, *Essai sur les origines du lexique technique de la mystique musulmane*, (Paris, 1922), 124 ff.

3. Ibn Sacd, *Kitāb aṭ-ṭabaqāt al-kubrā*, ed. E. Sachau et al. (Leiden, 1909–40), 9 vols, 5:153.

4. Abū Nucaym al-Iṣfahānī, *Ḥilyat al-auliyā*, Cairo 1351 ff. H/1932, 10 vols, 6:310. Hereafter *Ḥilya*.

5. *Ḥilya* 2:103 f.

6. *Ḥilya* 2:96.

7. *Ḥilya* 2:208.

8. *Ḥilya* 9:372.

9. *Ḥilya* 10:11, 181.

10. Abū'd-Dardā, in ash-Sha^cranī, *Lawāqiḥ al-anwār*, Cairo 1299 H/1883, 2 vols., 1:31: *Ḥilya* 3:19 from Yūnus ibn ^cUbayd; ibd. 7:70 from Sufyān ath-Thaurī.

11. Abū Ḥāmid al-Ghazālī, *Iḥyā' ^culūm ad-dīn*, Cairo 1334H/1915-16, 4 vols.; 4:291.

12. *Ḥilya* 10:152.

13. *Ḥilya* 2:365; as tradition from one of his disciples ibd. 7:135. (The word *furqān* (lit. 'discernment', also a designation for the Qur'ān] means here 'revelation', *GW*).

14. *Ḥilya* 10:5.

15. *Ḥilya* 6:29. (*Ḥanīf*, probably from Syrian *ḥanpa*, is the designation of an ascetic who does not belong to the Islamic community but to the primordial monotheistic religion, *GW*). [For a discussion of its various meanings see *Encyclopedia of Islam*, 2nd edition, vol. 3: 165–66].

16. at-Tirmidhī, *Nawādir al-uṣūl*, Istanbul 1293H/1876, 7.

17. *Ḥilya* 6:121.

18. Translator's note: The Swedish original here makes reference to the Blocksberg. The author alludes to Mount Brocken in the Harz mountains in Germany, where witches and warlocks were traditionally believed to assemble, particularly on May 1.

19. ash-Sha^cranī, *Lawāqiḥ al-anwār* 1:80.

20. *Ḥilya* 4:226, 314; cf. ibid. 6:112.

21. ash-Sha^cranī, *Lawāqiḥ al-anwār* 1:80.

22. *Ḥilya* 7:23.

23. As *ḥadīth* in at-Tirmidhī, *Nawādir al-uṣūl* 17; as word from ^cUbayd ibn ^cUmar: *Ḥilya* 3:[2]73.

24. [al-Ghazālī, *Iḥyā' ^culūm ad-dīn* 4:204 (not: *Ḥilya*)].

25. [al-Ghazālī, *Iḥyā' ^culūm ad-dīn* 4:362 (not: *Ḥilya*)].

26. ath-Tha^clabī, *^cArā'is al-majālis*, Cairo 1303 H/1886–7, 272.

27. *Ḥilya* 7:301.

28. *Ḥilya* 6:53.

29. *Ḥilya* 6:328.

30. *Ḥilya* 2:383. [The story has been elaborated by the Persian poet Niẓāmī, and was introduced into German literature by Goethe in the *Noten und*

Abhandlungen zum West-Östlichen Divan, "Allgemeines", as a model of poetic style.]

31. al-Jāḥiẓ, *Kitāb Bayān at-tabyīn*, [no edition given; the Cairo edition of 1367 H/1948-9, cannot have been used by Andrae], 2:91: Cf. St. Mark 9:12.

32. *Ḥilya* 7:148 [read: *Hilya* 8:147].

33. Abū Ṭālib al-Makkī, *Qūt al-qulūb*, Cairo 1310/1892-3, 2 vols. 2:74.

34. *Ḥilya* 2:382.

35. *Ḥilya* 7:299.

36. ath-Thaᶜlabī, *ᶜArā'is al-majālis* 251.

37. al-Jāḥiẓ, *Kitāb Bayān at-tabyīn* 2:91.

38. *Ḥilya* 6:181.

39. H.S. Nyberg, ["Några utvecklingslinjer i Muhammads religiöse förkunnelse"] in *Religion och Bibel*, 4 (1945), 30–40.

40. *Ḥilya* 6: 23, 28 f.; [for Kaᶜb see *Encyclopedia of Islam*, 2nd. edition, 4:316–17].

41. *Ḥilya* 6:5–10.

42. *Ḥilya* 5:378.

43. *Ḥilya* 5:365.

44. *Ḥilya* 5:387.

45. *Ḥilya* 2:128.

46. *Ḥilya* 6:45.

47. *Ḥilya* 4:9 [?; but cf. ibid. 4:99!].

48. adh-Dhahabī, *Tadhkirat al-ḥuffāẓ*, Hyderabad 1333H/1915, 1:49.

49. *Ḥilya* 4:24.

50. *Ḥilya* 4:33.

51. *Ḥilya* 4:24, cf. also adh-Dhahabī, *Tadhkirat al-ḥuffāẓ* 1:95.

52. R. Reitzenstein, *Historia Monachorum*, Göttingen 1916, 193.

53. Palladius, *The Paradise of the Fathers*, transl. E.W.Budge, 2:63.

54. *Ḥilya* 4:44.

55. *Ḥilya* 4:49.

56. Palladius, *The Paradise of the Fathers*, 2:111.

57. ath-Tha[c]labī, ʿArāʾ*is-majālis* 276, 281.

58. In an account of the different kinds of sciences in which az-Zuhrī was a master, there are mentioned, among others, poetry, genealogy of the Arabs, Qur'an, Sunna, along with "traditions about prophets and the People of the Book," *Ḥilya* 3:361.

59. The quotations from the Gospel in my sources are: *St. Matthew* 4:37, 5:6; 5:7; 5:13; 5:19; 5:24–25; 5:27; 5:41–44; 6:3; 6:17; 6:19–20; 6:26; 7:2; 7:6; 7:14, 7:15; 7:16 (eight times!): 9:12; 10:8; 10:16; 10:39; 11:17; 12:30; 16:25; 19:21–24; 26:39; *St. Mark* 12.41–44; *St. Luke* 11, 27–28; 12:15–21; 22:44; *St. John* 8:7.

60. al-Ghazālī, *Iḥyāʾ [c]ulūm ad-dīn* 4:177.

61. *Ḥilya* 3:67.

62. *Ḥilya* 5:240 f.

63. *Ḥilya* 6:115.

64. *Ḥilya* 4:119.

65. *Ḥilya* 8:146.

66. *Ḥilya* 4:38f; cf. al-Jāḥiẓ, *Kitāb Bayān at-tabyīn* 2:91.

67. *Ḥilya* 10:136.

68. *Ḥilya* 10:197.

69. al-Jāḥiẓ, *Kitāb Bayān at-tabyīn*, 2:88.

70. as-Sulamī, *Ṭabaqāt aṣ-ṣūfīya*, WE 139 fol. 16 b [= ed. Sharība, 105. The translation should rather be "your *nafs*, your lower self"].

71. Tor Andrae, "Zuhd und Mönchtum", *Le Monde Oriental* (50) 1931: 296–327.

72. as-Sulamī, *Ṭabaqāt aṣ-ṣūfīya*, WE fol. 15 b [= ed. Sharība, 101, attributed to Aḥmad ibn Abīʾl-Ḥawārī].

73. Chwolson, *Die Sabier*, St. Petersburg 1856, 2:373. Chwolson translated *ta'allaha* as 'worship.'

74. G. Henrici, *Die Hermesmystik und das Neue Testament*, Leipzig 1918, 59.

75. Ibn al- Jauzī, *Ṣifat aṣ-ṣafwa*, MS. Berlin, Cod. Wetzstein (WE) 24, fol. 2 b.

76. *Ḥilya* 6:379.

77. *Ḥilya* 9:351.

78. Margaret Smith, *Studies in early mysticism*, (London, 1931), 250; [for Muḥāsibi see Josef van Ess, *Die Gedankenwelt des al-Ḥāritt al-Muḥāsibī*, Bonn 1957].

79. *Ḥilya*, MS. Berlin, codex Landberg, 984, fol. 262b.

80. *Ḥilya* 10:151.

81. Hujwīrī, *Kashf* 409.

Chapter II

1. ash-Shaᶜrānī, *Lawāqiḥ al-anwār* 1:38; as word from Hishām: *Ḥilya* 6:269. [For Ḥasan al-Baṣrī see Hellmut Ritter, "Studien zur islamischen Frömmigkeit," *Der Islam* 21 (1933).]

2. Ibn al-Jauzī, *Ṣifat aṣ-ṣafwa*, WE 24, fol. 26b.

3. al-Qushayrī, *Ar-Risāla fī't-taṣawwuf*, at the margin of ᶜArūsī's *Natā'ij al-afkār*, 1:71.

4. ash-Shaᶜrānī, *Lawāqiḥ al-anwār* 1:92.

5. ash-Shaᶜrānī, *Lawāqiḥ al-anwār* 1:93.

6. *Ḥilya* 8:243.

7. al-Makkī, *Qūt al-qulūb* 2:295.

8. al-Makkī, *Qūt al-qulūb* 2:289.

9. *Ḥilya* 10:124.

10. al-Makkī, *Qūt al-qulūb* 2:289.

11. Ibn Adham: *Ḥilya* 8:34.

12. al-Ghazālī, *Iḥyā' ᶜulūm* ad-dīn 2:82.

13. al-Makkī, *Qūt al-qulūb* 2:289.

14. Ibn al-Jauzī, *Ṣifat aṣ-ṣafwa*, WE 24, fol. 20b.

15. ash-Shaᶜrāni, *Lawāqiḥ al-anwār* 1:105. Muḥāsibī knew a similar sign of warning: *Ḥilya* 10:75.

16. al-Makkī, *Qūt al-qulūb* 2:291.

17. Ibn al-Jauzī, *Ṣifat aṣ-ṣafwa* WE 24, fol. 16a.

18. *Ḥilya* 8:298.

19. *Ḥilya* 8:293 [read: 353; another story about Bishr and his work in spinning in al-Ghazālī, *Iḥyā' ᶜulūm ad-dīn* 4:232].

20. al-Makkī, *Qūt al-qulūb* 2:296.

21. *Ḥilya* 3:279 [?].

22. Ibn al-Jauzī, *Ṣifat aṣ-ṣafwa* WE 24, fol. 21 b.

23. al-Makkī, *Qūt al-qulūb* 2:287.

24. ash-Sha^{c}rānī, *Lawāqiḥ al-anwār* [no page number!].

25. al-Makkī, *Qūt al-qulūb* 2:274.

26. al-Ghazālī, *Iḥyā' ^{c}ulūm ad-dīn* 2:82.

27. About similar ideas even inside Christian monastic piety see Tor Andrae, *Zuhd und Mönchtum*, 300.

28. Ibn al-Jauzī, *Ṣifat aṣ-ṣafwa*, WE 25, fol. 183a.

29. al-Ghazālī, *Iḥyā' ^{c}ulūm ad-dīn* 2:204.

30. al-Makkī, *Qūt al-qulūb* 2:291.

31. al-Makkī, *Qūt al-qulūb* 2:238.

32. al-Makkī, *Qūt al-qulūb* 2:255.

33. al-Makkī, *Qūt al-qulūb* 2:239.

34. *Ḥilya* 6:11.

35. al-Makkī, *Qūt al-qulūb* 2:239.

36. ash-Sha^{c}rānī, *Lawāqiḥ al-anwār* 1:39.

37. ash-Sha^{c}rānī, *Lawāqiḥ al-anwār* 1:38.

38. *Ḥilya* 2:234.

39. ash-Sha^{c}rānī, *Lawāqiḥ al-anwār* 1:57.

40. *Ḥilya* 2:365.

41. *Ḥilya* 2:366.

42. *Ḥilya* 2:380.

43. *Ḥilya* 2:359; Cf. ash-Sha^{c}rānī, *Lawāqiḥ al-anwār* 1:61.

44. Ibn al-Jauzī, *Ṣifat aṣ-ṣafwa*, WE 25 fol. 133 b.

45. *Ḥilya* 8:41.

46. al-Ghazālī, *Ihyā' ^{c}ulūm ad-dīn* 4:299.

47. *Ḥilya* 6:195.

48. *Ḥilya* 7:75.

49. *Ḥilya* 6:12.

50. al-Makkī, *Qūt al-qulūb* 2:237.

51. *Ḥilya* 8:269.

52. *Ḥilya* 3:131.

53. al-Makkī, *Qūt al-qulūb* 2:238 ff.

54. al-Makkī, *Qūt al-qulūb* 2:241.

55. Translator's note: Fredrik Troels-Lund (b. 1840), Danish historian and author of a fourteen-volume work in Danish, *Daily Life in Scandinavia in the Sixteenth Century.*

56. al-Makkī, *Qūt al-qulūb* 2:245.

57. al-Makkī, *Qūt al-qulūb* 2:57; [cf. the story about the stern ascetic Ibn Khafīf (d. 982) that he saw in his dream, a child guiding his parents across the Sirāṭ-bridge, and he immediately married in order to be blessed with such a help at Doomsday; Farīduddīn ᶜAṭṭār, *Tadhkirat al-auliyā*, ed. Reynold A. Nicholson, (London-Leiden 1905–1907), 2 vols., 2:128.]

58. ash-Shaᶜrānī, *Lawāqiḥ al-anwār* 1:64, 61.

59. al-Ghazālī, *Iḥyā' ᶜulūm ad-dīn* 2:29.

60. ash-Shaᶜrānī, *Lawāqiḥ al-anwār* 1:99.

61. al-Ghazālī, *Iḥyā' ᶜulūm ad-dīn* 2:22.

62. al-Qushayrī, *Risāla* 1:207.

63. al-Ghazālī, *Iḥyā' ᶜulūm ad-dīn* 4:232.

64. al-Makkī, *Qūt al-qulūb* 2:241.

65. al-Makkī, *Qūt al-qulūb* 2:238.

66. al-Makkī, *Qūt al-qulūb* 2:259.

67. *Ḥilya*, cod. Landberg 984, fol. 261b.

68. *Ḥilya*, cod. Landberg 984, fol. 257a.

69. al-Ghazālī, *Iḥyā' ᶜulūm ad-dīn* 2:22.

70. al-Ghazālī, *Iḥyā' ᶜulūm ad-dīn* 2:36, 4:206.

71. al-Ghazālī, *Iḥyā' ᶜulūm ad-dīn* 2:22; as saying of Sahl at-Tustarī in: Abū Ḥafṣ ᶜUmar as-Suhrawardī, *ᶜAwārif al-maᶜārif*, at the margin of al-Ghazālī, *Iḥyā' ᶜulūm ad-dīn* 2:266.

72. *Ḥilya*, cod. Landberg 984, fol. 262 a.

73. [One can barely call the relation between Aḥmad ibn Abī'l-Ḥawārī and Rābiᶜa a "spiritual marriage"; Rābiᶜa had close spiritual relationships with almost all the leading Sufis of her time].

74. as-Sulamī, *Ṭabaqāt aṣ-ṣūfīya*, WE 139, fol. 13 a [= ed. Sharība, 93, where only the first half of the saying about the four deaths is found].

75. ash-Shaᶜrānī, *Lawāqiḥ al-anwār* 1:105.

76. al-Makkī, *Qūt al-qulūb* 1:269.

77. al-Makkī, *Qūt al-qulūb* 269.

78. at-Tirmidhī, *Nawādir al-uṣūl* 24 [Stories about the poverty of ᶜAlī ibn Abī Ṭālib and his family abound in Shia sources and poetry].

79. al-ᶜArūsī, *Natā'ij al-afkār* 1:114.

80. Translator's note: Georg Stiernhielm (1590–1672), poet, scholar and civil servant. Witty and tolerant, Stiernhielm has been called a typical literary representative of the period of Sweden's great power in Europe.

81. al-Ghazālī, *Iḥyā ᶜulūm ad-dīn* 4:206.

82. al-Makkī, *Qūt al-qulūb* 2:247.

83. [*Ḥilya* 5:236 (not: *Iḥyā'!*). In Sanā'ī's (d. 1131) Persian poem *Ḥadīqat al-ḥaqīqa*, ed. Mudarris Rižavi, (Teheran, 1950), 271, one pious woman is said to receive the recompense of a thousand men!].

84. Hujwīrī, *Kashf* 120. [For the whole problem see Margaret Smith, *Rābiᶜa the Mystic, and her fellow saints in Islam*, (Cambridge, 1928, repr. 1984); and Annemarie Schimmel, *Mystical Dimensions of Islam*, (Chapel Hill, 1975), Appendix 2].

85. ash-Shaᶜrānī, *Lawāqiḥ al-anwār* 1:93.

86. al ᶜArūsī, *Natā'ij al-afkār* 1:114.

87. *Ḥilya* cod. Landberg 984, fol. 265 a.

88. *Ḥilya* cod. Landberg 984, fol. 261 a.

89. al-Makkī, *Qūt al-qulūb* 2:139.

90. *Ḥilya* cod. Landberg 984, fol. 257 a.

91. as-Sulamī, *Ṭabaqāt aṣ-ṣūfīya*, WE 139, fol. 17 b. [Not in ed. Sharība. The saying that the infidel eats with seven stomachs is a *ḥadīth* mentioned by al-Bukhārī, see B. Furūzānfar, *Aḥādīth-i Mathnavī*, (Teheran 1950), No. 449; it is also cited by al-Ghazālī and other authors.]

92. al-ᶜArūsī, *Natā'ij al-afkār* 1:110.

93. al-Ghazālī, *Iḥyā' ᶜulūm ad-dīn* 3:72.

94. ash-Shaᶜrānī, *Lawāqiḥ al-anwār* 1:93.

95. as-Suhrawardi, *ᶜAwārif al-maᶜārif* 2:138.

96. al-Ghazālī, *Iḥyā' ᶜulūm ad-dīn* 2:16.

97. ash-Shaᶜrānī, *Lawāqiḥ al-anwār* I:94. [A late story about Junayd tells also that he, as a boy refused to eat in order to avoid to go to the latrine out of shame, as "God is present and watching." See Muḥammad al-Ḥusaynī Gēsūdarāz, *Jawāmi ᶜal-Kilam*, (Cawnpore, 1937), s.v. 11. Shaᶜbān 802.

98. al-Ghazālī, *Iḥyā' ᶜulūm ad-dīn* 4:349.

99. *Ḥilya* 10:110.

100. ash-Shaᶜrānī, *Lawāqiḥ al-anwār* 1:98.

101. *Ḥilya* cod. Landberg 984, fol. 260 b.

102. *Ḥilya*, 10:39.

103. ash-Shaᶜrānī, *Lawāqiḥ al-anwār* 1:102.

104. ash-Shaᶜrānī, *Lawāqiḥ al-anwār* 1:105.

105. *Ḥilya*, cod. Landberg 984, fol. 59 a.

106. *Ḥilya* 6:19.

Chapter III

1. *Ḥilya* 9:385–86.

2. *Ḥilya* 9:340, 345, 380–81.

3. Ibn ᶜArabī, *Muḥāḍarāt al-abrār*, (Cairo, 1305 H/1887–8), 2 vols., 1:81, cf. 133.

4. *Ḥilya* , cod. Landberg 984, fol. 50 a.

5. ash-Shaᶜrānī, *Lawāqiḥ al-anwār* 1:113.

6. Ibn al-Jauzī, *Ṣifat aṣ-ṣafwa*, WE 25, fol. 176 a; al-Jāḥiẓ, *Kitāb Bayān at-tabyīn* 2:101; al-Ghazālī, *Iḥyā' ᶜulūm ad-dīn* 2:208, among many others.

7. *Ḥilya* 7:[342, 353].

8. al-Ghazālī, *Iḥyā' ᶜulūm ad-dīn* 2:198.

9. *Ḥilya* 9:380.

10. as-Sulamī, *Ṭabaqāt aṣ-ṣūfīya*, WE 139, fol 17 b [= ed. Sharība 112. One would rather translate that these pious people "have no *uns*, friendly relation, intimacy, with other people.]

11. *Ḥilya* 10:60.

12. *Ḥilya* , cod. Landberg 984, fol. 265 a.

13. as-Sulamī, *Ṭabaqāt aṣ-ṣūfīya*, WE 139, fol. 25 a [= ed. Sharība 139].

14. Palladius, *The Paradise of the Fathers* 2: 1; 47.

15. al-Ghazālī, *Iḥyā' ᶜulūm ad-dīn* 2:204.

16. al-Ghazālī, *Iḥyā' ᶜulūm ad-dīn* 2:198.

17. al-Ghazālī, *Iḥyā' ᶜulūm ad-dīn* 4:209.

18. Ibn al-Jauzī, *Ṣifat aṣ-ṣafwa*, WE 24, fol. 117 b.

19. Ibn al-Jauzī, *Ṣifat aṣ-ṣafwa*, WE 24, fol. 118 a.

20. al-Ghazālī, *Iḥyā' ᶜulūm ad-dīn* 4:98 [?].
21. as-Suhrawardī, *ᶜAwārif al-maᶜārif* 4:157.
22. al-Ghazālī, *Iḥyā' ᶜulūm ad-dīn* 2:153.
23. al-Ghazālī, *Iḥyā' ᶜulūm ad-dīn* 2:159.
24. al-Ghazālī, *Iḥyā' ᶜulūm ad-dīn* 2:153.
25. *Ḥilya*, cod. Landberg 984, fol. 53 a.
26. *Ḥilya* 10:357.
27. Ibn al-Jauzī, *Ṣifat aṣ-ṣafwa*, WE 24, fol. 3 b, 5 b.
28. al-Ghazālī, *Iḥyā' ᶜulūm ad-dīn* [2:162].
29. *Ḥilya* 10:255–56.
30. Ibn Saᶜd, *Kitāb aṭ-ṭabaqāt al-kubrā* 6:132.
31. *Ḥilya*, cod. Landberg 984, fol. 22 b.
32. as-Sulamī, *Ṭabaqāt aṣ-ṣūfīya*, WE 139, fol. 22 b (not in ed. Sharība].
33. *Ḥilya* 10:276–77.
34. *Ḥilya* 10:117.
35. *Ḥilya* 10:137.
36. *Ḥilya* 10:84–85.
37. *Ḥilya*, cod. Landberg 984, fol. 253 a.
38. *Ḥilya*, cod. Landberg 984, fol. 264 a.
39. *Ḥilya* 10:18.
40. *Ḥilya* 8:22.
41. *Ḥilya*, cod. Landberg 984, fol. 265 a.
42. al-Makkī, *Qūt al-qulūb* 2:249.
43. al-Makkī, *Qūt al-qulūb* 2:250.
44. al-Makkī, *Qūt al-qulūb* 2:267.
45. *Ḥilya* 8:28.
46. *Ḥilya* 6:371, 388.
47. *Ḥilya* 8:21.
48. *Ḥilya* 8:21–22.
49. *Ḥilya* 7 [:367].

50. *Ḥilya* 7:371.

51. *Ḥilya* 7:370.

52. Ibn al-Jauzī, *Ṣifat aṣ-ṣafwa*, WE 24, fol. 19 a.

53. *Ḥilya* 7:373.

54. *Ḥilya* 7:385.

55. *metta* is the Buddhist term for charity. *GW*

56. [*Ḥilya* 7:] 373.

57. al-Makkī, *Qūt al-qulūb* 1:244.

58. *Ḥilya* 10:55; *Ḥilya*, cod. Landberg 984 fol. 260 a.

59. al-Makkī, *Qūt al-qulūb* 1:246–47; cf. ash-Sha^{c}rānī, *Lawāqiḥ al-anwār* 1:39.

60. al-Ghazālī, *Iḥyā' ^{c}ulūm ad-dīn* 4:209 [saying of Yaḥyā ibn Mu^{c}ādh].

61. *Ḥilya*, cod. Landberg 984, fol. 259 a.

62. *Ḥilya* 10:54 [This saying occurs in a *ḥadīth* and is usually ascribed to Jesus; it is written at the entrance gate of Akbar's residence Fathpur Sikri].

63. Zakariya al-Anṣārī, *Sharḥ ar-Risāla al-Qushayriyya*, at the margin of al-^{c}Arūsī, *Natā'ij al-afkār*, 1:122.

64. al-Qushayrī, *Risāla*, 1:120.

65. Thomas a Kempis, *Imitatio Christi*, trans. Leo Sherley-Price, (Penguin Classics, 1952), 2:4 (translator's note).

66. *Ḥilya* 10:64.

67. *Ḥilya* 10:54.

68. al-Ghazālī, *Iḥyā' ^{c}ulūm ad-dīn* 2:220; *Ḥilya* 10:126.

69. *Ḥilya* 9:342.

70. Translator's note: The author probably refers to a Swedish translation of selected letters from Tagore 1885–1895, published in Swedish as *Glimtar från Bengalen*, 1921.

71. *Ḥilya* 9:355.

72. *Ḥilya* 9:399.

73. *Ḥilya* 10:64–66.

74. *Ḥilya* cod. Landberg 984, fol. 257 b.

75. at-Tirmidhī, *Nawādir al-uṣūl* 64.

76. *Ḥilya* 10:284–87.

Chapter IV

1. *Ḥilya*, cod. Landberg 984, fol. 60 a.

2. as-Suhrawardī, *ᶜAwārif al-maᶜārif* 4:102.

3. Hujwīrī, *Kashf* 359.

4. *Ḥilya* 9:356–57. [The story is well known, but is not found in this account of Dhū'n-Nūn].

5. as-Suhrawardī. *ᶜAwārif al-maᶜārif* 4:149 f.

6. as-Suhrawardī, *ᶜAwārif al-ma ᶜārif* 4:159.

7. as-Suhrawardī, *ᶜAwārif al-maᶜārif* 3:100 f.

8. al-Ghazālī, *Iḥyā' ᶜulūm ad-dīn* 2:211.

9. *Ḥilya* 10:118 f.

10. al-Ghazālī, *Iḥyā' ᶜulūm ad-dīn* 3:26.

11. *Ḥilya* 10: 148.

12. *Ḥilya* 9:364–65 Therefore *maᶜrifa* can be equated sometimes with *ilhām*, ['inspiration']; see Louis Massignon, *Textes hallagiennes* 202 [*Essai sur les origines du lexique technique* 224].

13. ash-Shaᶜrānī, *Lawāqiḥ al-anwār* 1:105.

14. *Ḥilya*, cod. Landberg 984, fol. 260 a.

15. al-Ghazālī, *Iḥyā' ᶜulūm ad-dīn* 2:126 [?].

16. *Ḥilya*, cod. Landberg 984, fol. 252 a.

17. *Ḥilya*, cod. Landberg 984, fol. 263 a.

18. as-Sulamī, *Ṭabaqāt aṣ-ṣūfīya*, WE 139, fol. 8 a [ed. Sharība 26].

19. ash-Shaᶜrānī, *Lawāqiḥ al-anwār* 1:94.

20. ash-Shaᶜrānī, *Lawāqiḥ al-anwār* 1:94.

21. *Ḥilya* 10: 257–59.

22. *Ḥilya* 10:235 [?].

23. *Ḥilya* 9:371.

24. Hujwīrī, *Kashf* 182.

25. *Ḥilya*, cod. Landberg 984, fol. 259 a.

26., al-ᶜArūsī, *Natā'ij al-afkār* 1:140.

27. *Ḥilya* 10: 261–62 [?].

28. *Ḥilya* 9:[3] 59–60.

29. *Ḥilya* 9:374.

30. *Ḥilya* 10:64.

31. al-Ghazālī, *Iḥyā' ᶜulūm ad-dīn* 4:43 [For Sahl at-Tustarī see: Gerhard Böwering, *The Mystical Vision of Existence in Classical Islam. The Qur'ānic Hermeneutics of the Sufi Sahl at-Tustarī (d. 283/896)*, Berlin-New York, 1980.

32. *Ḥilya* 10:35.

33. as-Suhrawardī, *ᶜAwārif al-maᶜārif* 4:369.

34. Ibn al-Jauzī, *Ṣifat aṣ-ṣafwa*, WE 24, fol. 118 b.

35. Translator's note: Carl Olof Rosenius (1816–1868), Swedish lay evangelist and founder in 1856 of the Methodist-inspired "Evangeliska Fosterlandsstiftelsen" (Evangelical National Missionary Society).

36. al-Qushayrī, *Risāla* 1:144.

37. al-Ghazālī, *Iḥyā' ᶜulūm ad-dīn* 2:266.

38. *Ḥilya* 6:271; as saying of Abū'd-Dardā' in ash-Shaᶜrānī, *Lawāqiḥ al-anwār* 1:31.

39. *Ḥilya* 8:17.

40. al-Ghazālī, *Iḥyā' ᶜulūm ad-dīn* 4:362.

41. *Ḥilya*, cod. Landberg 984, fol. 60 a.

42. al-Ghazālī, *Iḥyā' ᶜulūm ad-dīn* 4:361–71.

43. *Ḥilya* 8:17.

44. *Ḥilya*, cod. Landberg 984, fol. 256 a.

45. al-Ghazālī, *Iḥyā' ᶜulūm ad-dīn* 4:264.

46. *Ḥilya* 7:218.

47. ad-Damīrī, *Ḥayāt al-ḥayawān* (Cairo, 1330), vol. 2 [= Cairo 1376H/1956 2:119 ff. s.v. *fākhta*].

48. *Ḥilya*, cod. Landberg. 984, fol. 257 a.

49. For extensive discussion of the Sufis' attitude in this respect see Hujwīrī, *Kashf* 393 ff; al-Sarrāj, *Kitāb al-lumaᶜ [fī't-taṣawwuf*, ed. Reynold A. Nicholson, (London-Leiden, 1914)], 186 f; 267 ff; al-Qushayrī, *Risāla*, ed. (Cairo, 1318 H/1900–1), 178 ff; cf. also Duncan Black MacDonald, "Emotional Religion in Islam as Affected by Music and Singing," *Journal of the Royal Asiatic Society* 1901, 1902; [further: Fritz Meier, "Der Derwischtanz" *Asiatische Studien* 8 (1954); Marijan Molé, "La Danse exstatique en Islam", in: *Sources Orientales* 6, (Paris, 1963): Annemarie Schimmel, *Mystical Dimensions of Islam*, 178–86].

50. al-Ghazālī, *Iḥyā' ᶜulūm ad-dīn* 2:259.

51. *Ḥilya* 9:354.

52. as-Sulamī, *Ṭabaqāt aṣ-ṣūfīya*, WE 139, fol. 19 b [= ed. Sharība, 119].

53. *Ḥilya* 10:271.

54. al-ᶜArūsī, *Natā'ij al-afkār* 1:141.

55. al-ᶜArūsī, *Natā'ij al-afkār* 1:141.

56. as-Suhrawardī, *ᶜAwārif al-maᶜārif* 2:212; cf. al-Ghazālī, *Iḥyā' ᶜulūm ad-dīn* 2:265.

57. *Ḥilya* 3:69.

58. [Massignon, *Essai sur les origines du lexique technique . . .*, 209–10].

59. *Ḥilya* 10:61 [Yaḥyā ibn Muᶜadh].

60. *Ḥilya*, cod. Landberg 984, fol. 265 b.

61. *Ḥilya* 6:69.

62. *Ḥilya* 2:190.

63. Ibn al-Jauzī, *Ṣifat aṣ-ṣafwa*, WE 24, fol. 67 b.

64. Ibn al-Jauzī, *Ṣifat aṣ-ṣafwa*, WE 25, fol. 56 a.

65. al-Ghazālī, *Iḥyā' ᶜulūm ad-dīn* 4:351.

66. Ibn al-Jauzī, *Ṣifat aṣ-ṣafwa*, WE 24, fol. 69 b.

67. *Ḥilya* 9:383.

68. Aphraates, *Homilien*, transl. by G. Bert, 148.

69. *Ḥilya* 9:342–43.

70. *Ḥilya* 9:336 [Incorrect; this would be the biography of Dhū'n-Nūn. But the story is not found in the biographies of Bāyezīd Bisṭāmī and Yaḥyā ibn Muᶜādh either, as they are recorded in *Ḥilya* 10:33–42 and 10:42–70 respectively].

Chapter V

1. *Ḥilya* 5:19; 7:61. Rabīᶜa and Muḍar were two north Arabian tribes. *GW*.

2. Iblīs is the Arabic name of the devil. One thinks that the term is derived from Greek *diabolos*. *GW* [For a discussion about Iblīs in Sufi psychology see Peter J. Awn, *Satan's Fall and Redemption* (Leiden, 1982)].

3. *Ḥilya* 10:205.

4. *Ḥilya* [8]: 64–65.

5. al-Ghazālī, *Iḥyā' ᶜulūm ad-dīn* 4:112.

6. *Ḥilya* 10:272–73.

7. as-Sulamī, *Ṭabaqāt aṣ-ṣūfīya*, WE 139, fol. 14 [ed. Sharība 96).

8. ash-Sha^c^rānī, *Lawāqiḥ al-anwār* 1:107.

9. Hujwīrī, *Kashf*, [109–] 110; [cf. for a modern interpretation of the motif Muhammad Iqbal, *Jāvīdnāma*, Sphere of Jupiter, "Satan's Complaint," (Lahore, 1932); Engl. translation by Arthur J. Arberry (London, 1966)].

10. ash-Sha^c^rānī, *Lawāqiḥ al-anwār* 1:112.

11. *Ḥilya* cod. Landberg 984, fol. 254 b.

12. *Ḥilya* 10:122.

13. al-Jāḥiz, *Kitāb Bayān at-tabyīn* 2:95.

14. *Ḥilya*, cod. Landberg 984, fol. 266 b.

15. Margaret Smith, [*Rābi^c^a the Mystic*, 99].

16. Ibn al-Jauzī, *Ṣifat aṣ-ṣafwa*, WE 25 fol. 132 b.

17. ash-Sha^c^rānī, *Lawāqiḥ al-anwār* 1:44 [probably developed out of the Qur'anic word *yā laytanī kuntu turāban*, "I wish I were dust," (Sura 78:41)—the exclamation at Doomsday of the infidels].

18. *Ḥilya*, cod. Landberg 984 fol. 57 a.

19. Ibn al-Jauzī, *Ṣifat aṣ-ṣafwa*, WE 24 fol. 3 a.

20. Ibn al-Jauzī, *Ṣifat aṣ-ṣafwa*, WE 24 fol. 4 a.

21. *Ḥilya* 9: 336.

22. *Ḥilya* 9:388–90 [The translation, which is not absolutely literal but captures the content and style very well, begins with verse 8 and leaves out the last three verses].

23. The description of the four figures certainly goes back, in the last instance, to Ezekiel 10:14, where a cherub is mentioned instead of an animal. But the Hebrew word for cherub is the same as the Babylonian *karuba*, which means mediator, and is sometimes used for the winged animal figures that were placed at the entrance doors of palaces and temples as protecting deities. The basis for the idea that animals are intercessors for their respective races is Iranian, expressed in *Yasna* 29, where the animal soul complains of the treatment to which bovines are exposed. For the same idea in other Islamic texts see Tor Andrae, *Die person Muhammads in lehre und glauben seiner gemeinde*, (Stockholm, 1918), 74. *GW*.

24. *Ḥilya* 9:374.

25. *Ḥilya* 9:373.

26. *Ḥilya* 10:63.

27. *Ḥilya* 10:53.

28. *Ḥilya* 9:273 [?].

29. *Ḥilya* 10:39.

30. *Ḥilya* 10:37.

31. ash-Shaᶜrānī, *Lawāqiḥ al-anwār* 1:103.

32. al-Ghazālī, *Iḥyā' ᶜulūm ad-dīn* 4:411.

33. *Ḥilya* 10:207.

34. *Ḥilya* 10:37.

35. al-Makkī, *Qūt al-qulūb* 2:87.

36. ash-Shaᶜrānī, *Lawāqiḥ al-anwār* 1:113.

37. *Ḥilya* 6:326.

38. *Ḥilya* 10:82.

39. Hujwīrī, *Kashf* 331.

40. Translator's note: Bushrod Shedden Taylor, (b. 1840), popularly known as "California Taylor" and author of such works as *Holy Fire, or How, Where and Why to Promote Revivals of Holiness* (1887) and *Death, Hell, and Judgment* (1900).

41. *Ḥilya*, cod. Landberg 984, fol. 257 b.

42. Ibn al-Jauzī, *Ṣifat aṣ-ṣafwa*, WE 25, fol. 23 b.

43. al-Ghazālī, *Iḥyā' ᶜulūm ad-din* 4:146.

44. *Ḥilya* 10:205.

45. *Ḥilya* 2:153.

46. *Ḥilya* 10:168.

47. Ibn al-Jauzī, *Ṣifat aṣ-ṣafwa*, WE 24, fol. 67 a.

48. *Ḥilya* 10:121.

49. *Ḥilya* 10:52.

50. *Ḥilya* 9:351.

51. *Ḥilya*, cod. Landberg 984, fol. 251 a.

52. *Ḥilya*, cod. Landberg 984, fol. 251 b.

53. al-Jāḥiẓ, *Kitāb bayān at- tabyīn* 2:101.

54. ash-Shaᶜrānī, *Lawāqiḥ al-anwār* 1:38.

55. *Ḥilya*, cod. Landberg 984, fol. 257 a.

56. al-Ghazālī, *Iḥyā' ^{c}ulūm ad-dīn* 4:13.

57. al-Makkī, *Qūt al-qulūb* 2:62; [al-Ghazālī, *Iḥyā' ^{c}ulūm ad-dīn 4:132*].

58. *Ḥilya*, cod. Landberg 984, fol. 260 a.

59. as-Suhrawardī, *^{c}Awārif al-ma^{c}ārif* 4:317.

60. as-Suhrawardī, *^{c}Awārif al-ma^{c}ārif* 4:320; [al-Makkī, *Qūt al-qulūb* 2:58 ff; as-Sarrāj, *Kitāb al-luma fī't-taṣawwuf* 62, and many other instances].

61. al-Ghazālī, *Iḥyā' ^{c}ulūm ad-dīn* 4:141.

62. al-Makkī, *Qūt al-qulūb* 1:189.

63. as-Suhrawardī, *^{c}Awārif al-ma^{c}ārif* 4:290.

64. *Ḥilya* 10–239.

65. Translator's note: The Swedish text here quotes a line from a hymn: "Det står alltsammans i Guds nåd, att saliga vi bliva"; an equivalent thought is found in this couplet from Robert Bridges' hymn text: "All my hope on God is founded."

66. al-Makkī, *Qūt al-qulūb* 2:138 ff.

67. al-Makkī, *Qūt al-qulūb* 2:138.

68. Delacroix, *Essai sur le mysticism spéculatif en Allemagne*, 41. *GW*.

69. al-Makkī, *Qūt al-qulūb* 2:138 ff.

70. *Ḥilya* 9: 384.

71. *Ḥilya* 10: 52.

72. Ibn al-Jauzī, *Ṣifat aṣ-ṣafwa*, WE 24, fol. 2 b.

73. *Ḥilya* 10:38.

74. Abū ^{c}Abdallāh ibn al-Jallā', in Ibn al-Jauzī, *Ṣifat aṣ-ṣafwa* WE 24, fol. 35 b.

75. al-Ghazālī, *Iḥyā' ^{c}ulūm ad-dīn* 2:204.

76. *Ḥilya* 10:274.

77. al-Ghazālī, *Iḥyā' ^{c}ulūm ad-dīn* 4:161.

Chapter VI

1. al-Makkī, *Qūt al-qulūb* 2:87–88.

2. *Ḥilya*, cod. Landberg 984, fol. 262 b.

3. *Ḥilya* 9:334.

4. *Ḥilya* 10:51–52.

5. as-Sulamī, *Ṭabaqāt aṣ-ṣūfīya*, WE 139, fol. 15 a [= ed. Sharība 101, Aḥmad ibn Abī'l-Ḥawārī]; in *Ḥilya* 10:7 this saying appears in a form which is apparently corrected according to Muḥāsibī's viewpoint.

6. *Ḥilya* 10: 76.

7. *Ḥilya* 10:34.

8. al-Ghazālī, *Iḥyā' ᶜulūm ad-dīn* 4:286.

9. al-ᶜArūsī, *Natā'ij al-afkār* 1:140.

10. al-Ghazālī, *Iḥyā' ᶜulūm ad-dīn* 4:304.

11. *Ḥilya* 10:256.

12. al-Ghazālī, *Iḥyā' ᶜulūm ad-dīn* 4:85.

13. al-Makkī, *Qūt al-qulūb* 2:2.

14. *Ḥilya* 10:196. [The most detailed study of the concept of *tawakkul* is Benedikt Reinert, *Die Lehre vom* tawakkul *in der älteren Sufik*, (Berlin, 1968)].

15. as-Suhrawardī, *ᶜAwārif al-maᶜārif* 4:323.

16. Ibn al-Jauzī, *Ṣifat aṣ-ṣafwa*, WE 25, fol. 179 b, 183 b.

17. al-Ghazālī, *Iḥyā' ᶜulūm ad-dīn* 4:211.

18. as-Sulamī, *Ṭabaqāt aṣ-ṣūfīya*, WE 139, fol. 35 b [= ed. Sharība 178].

19. al-Ghazālī, *Iḥyā' ᶜulūm ad-dīn* 2:227.

20. al-Makkī, *Qūt al-qulūb* 2:16.

21. *Ḥilya* 10:67.

22. as-Suhrawardī, *ᶜAwārif al-maᶜārif* 4:321–22.

23. al-Makkī, *Qūt al-qulūb* 2:136. [The use of the *istithnā*, 'taking exception', that is, to say *in shā'a Allāh*, God willing, is based on Qur'an Sura 68:18].

24. *Ḥilya* 9: [3]36–37.

25. al-Ghazālī, *Iḥyā' ᶜulūm ad-dīn* [4]: 297.

26. al-Ghazālī, *Iḥyā' ᶜulūm ad-dīn* 4:248.

27. Hujwīrī, *Kashf* 157.

28. al-Ghazālī, *Iḥyā' ᶜulūm ad-dīn* 4:245.

29. al-Ghazālī, *Iḥyā' ᶜulūm ad-dīn* 4:[2]32.

30. al-Makkī, *Qūt al-qulūb* 2:113 at the margin.

31. *Ḥilya* 10:192.

32. al-Makkī, *Qūt al-qulūb* 2:12.

33. ash-Shaᶜrānī, *Lawāqiḥ al-anwār* 1:112.

34. al-Ghazālī, *Iḥyā' ᶜulūm ad-dīn* 4:129 [?].

35. *Ḥilya*, cod. Landberg 984, fol. 45 b.

36. *Ḥilya*, cod. Landberg 984, fol. 257 a.

37. al-Ghazālī, *Iḥyā' ᶜulūm ad-dīn* 2:58.

38. al-Ghazālī, *Iḥyā' ᶜulūm ad-dīn* 2:77.

39. al-Qushayrī, *Risāla* 1:144.

40. al-Ghazālī, *Iḥyā' ᶜulūm ad-dīn* 2:76.

41. *Ḥilya* 10:280.

42. al-Ghazālī, *Iḥyā' ᶜulūm ad-dīn* 3:42.

43. al-Ghazālī, *Iḥyā' ᶜulūm ad-dīn* 4:16.

44. as-Sulamī, *Ṭabaqāt aṣ-ṣūfīya* WE 139, fol. 36 b [= ed. Sharība 182].

45. Sahl at-Tustarī: *Ḥilya* 10:54.

46. al-Ghazālī, *Iḥyā' ᶜulūm ad-dīn* 4:299; cf. *Ḥilya*, cod. Landberg 984, fol. 257 a.

47. al-ᶜArūsī, *Natā'ij al-afkār* 1:102.

48. Massignon, *La Passion d'al-Ḥosayn . . . al-Ḥallāj*, 2:608.

49. ash-Shaᶜrānī, *Lawāqiḥ al-anwār* 1:39.

50. *Ḥilya* [10:186, not] 9:86.

51. [But] cf. Ibn Adham, *Ḥilya* 8:36: "When you are alone with your friend, tear your shirt!" [A bridal mysticism comparable to that in Christian medieval Europe has developed only, to a certain extent, in the Indian subcontinent at a later period].

52. *Ḥilya* 10:34.

53. al-Makkī, *Qūt al-qulūb* 2:182.

54. *Ḥilya* 10:269.

55. *Ḥilya* 10:9.

56. *Ḥilya*, cod. Landberg 984, fol. 256 b.

57. as-Suhrawardī, *ᶜAwārif al-maᶜārif* 4:271. Wrongly ascribed to Dārānī in *Ḥilya*, cod. Landberg 984, fol. 255 a.

58. al-Ghazālī, *Iḥyā' ᶜulūm ad-dīn* 4:300.

59. as-Sulamī, *Ṭabaqāt aṣ-ṣūfīya* WE 139, fol. 37 b [= ed. Sharība 184. The verse has been quoted in almost all classical sources, and forms the basis of the later development of love mysticism].

60. [Andrae refers here to a poem by the German poet Heinrich Heine (1799–1856), who sings of the representatives of the *ḥubb ᶜudhrī*, a type of love praised in early Islamic times, which requires that the lover never attain to his goal. The members of the Arab tribe ᶜUdhrā were noted for this attitude—at least in theory. The attitude of dying from unrequited love is expressed in a *ḥadīth* ascribed to the Prophet:" Who loves and remains chaste and dies, dies as a martyr."].

61. *Ḥilya* 9:390.

62. *Ḥilya* 10:215 [? no verse of this kind is found there].

63. Ibn al-Jauzī, *Ṣifat aṣ-ṣafwa* WE 25, fol. 27 b.

64. al-Ghazālī, *Iḥyā' ᶜulūm ad-dīn* 4:308.

65. *Ḥilya* 10: 259–60.

66. *Ḥilya* 9:345.

67. *Ḥilya* 9:375.

68. as-Suhrawardī, *ᶜAwārif al-maᶜārif* 4:348.

69. al- ᶜArūsī, *Natā'ij al-afkār* 1:104.

70. al- ᶜArūsī, *Natā'ij al-afkār* 1:140 f.

71. al-Makkī, *Qūt al-qulūb* 2:77.

72. Translator's note: Sven Lidman (1882–1960) was prominent in the Pentecostal Revival movement in Sweden, and a writer of both secular and (following conversion) devotional literature.

73. al-Ghazālī, *Iḥyā' ᶜulūm ad-dīn* 4:272 ff.

74. Ibn al-Jauzī, *Ṣifat aṣ-ṣafwa* WE 24, fol. 3 a.

75. *Ḥilya* 10:35.

76. *Ḥilya*, cod. Landberg 984, fol. 253 a.

77. ash-Shaᶜrānī, *Lawāqiḥ al-anwār* 1:98.

78. *Ḥilya* 10:281.

79. Hujwīrī, *Kashf* 297.

80. as-Suhrawardī, *ᶜAwārif al-maᶜārif* 4:345.

81. *Ḥilya*, cod. Landberg 984, fol. 259 a.

82. *Ḥilya* 10:376.

83. as-Suhrawardī, *ᶜAwārif al-maᶜārif* 4:382.

84. as-Suhrawardī, *ᶜAwārif al-maᶜārif* 4:382.

INDEX OF PROPER NAMES

INDEX OF BOOKS AND ARTICLES

Index of Technical Terms